Augustus Hoppin

A Fashionable Sufferer

Chapters From Life's Comedy

Augustus Hoppin

A Fashionable Sufferer

Chapters From Life's Comedy

ISBN/EAN: 9783744664936

Printed in Europe, USA, Canada, Australia, Japan

Cover: Foto ©Thomas Meinert / pixelio.de

More available books at **www.hansebooks.com**

A FASHIONABLE SUFFERER

OR

Chapters from Life's Comedy

BY

AUGUSTUS HOPPIN
AUTHOR OF "RECOLLECTIONS OF AUTON HOUSE"

ILLUSTRATED BY THE AUTHOR

THIRD THOUSAND.

BOSTON
HOUGHTON, MIFFLIN AND COMPANY
New York: 11 East Seventeenth Street
The Riverside Press, Cambridge
1883

The Riverside Press, Cambridge:
Electrotyped and Printed by H. O. Houghton & Co.

PREFACE.

—◆—

I dedicate this work to the human influence which has caused me the sharpest pain and the keenest pleasure.

CONTENTS.

PROLOGUE.

ACT I.

Scene in a Large City. Time: Late Spring.

CHAPTER I.

CHAPTER II.

CHAPTER III.

CHAPTER IV.

ACT II.

Scene: "Paradise." Time: Summer Vacation.

CHAPTER I.

CHAPTER II.

CHAPTER III.

CHAPTER IV.

CHAPTER V.

CHAPTER VI.

EPILOGUE.

PROLOGUE,

IN WHICH THE OBJECT OF THE WORK IS SET FORTH, AND
THE PERSONS INTRODUCED.

HUMAN happiness is a cumulative sort of thing,—
scattered through life,—made up of sunshine and
ecstasy. Each bit, however, is a verity, possessing the component parts of delight, namely, a thrill,
and the subtle appreciation of it.

Human experience is composed in the same sort
of way : of individual sensations, which, in the ag-
gregate, form a complete existence. In childhood
we were delighted to peep through those small,
round, magnifying-glass apertures in the museum
which revealed to us the wonders of the world.
These glories, taken thus piecemeal, were more
fully appreciated than if they had been presented
in one great mass.

As it is much more instructive to study creation
in detail than in its more concrete capacity, so in
the following pages it is proposed to take a few
glimpses of life and character through the ideal
lens of experience. We shall materialize and in-
troduce to the reader a limited number of decently
dressed and " clever enough " individuals, and hear
what they have to say on various subjects.

Like everybody else nowadays, these fictitious people have their "peculiar views" which they desire to ventilate. Whether they are right or wrong, it is merely *their* way of looking at things, so nobody need be troubled about it.

Our purpose in thus proceeding is to show that the so-called "world" is simply a concrete totality of individual experiences; and to indicate that any one of these, however atomic, and apparently inconsequential, is never so unimportant as not to produce some sort of an impression on life.

The mimic stage upon which these ideal personages are to appear is, first, a certain corner in a certain street in a certain city; then, at the proper moment, the venue is changed to a blessed little "Paradise" among the green hills of Tucit-Kennoc, where the grass is greener, and the air purer than in many another spot which goes by the same sweet name. Here we shall dally until the first chill of autumn, listening to discussions on love and religion, on poetry, and other interesting topics. It is as if we were invited to pay a visit among a number of congenial friends in the country: as if we had packed portmanteau and dressing-case, and had actually proceeded to our destination; as if we had dwelt there during the summer heat, enjoying their intelligent conversation, and then had returned to town laden with pleasant reminiscences.

We shall endeavor to give to this episode the

smack of a comedy, without rigidly following the rules of such an arrangement, and, as intimated above, our attempt shall be confined to a few scenes in every-day life.

PERSONS INTRODUCED.

"THE BEAUTIFUL N. E.," *a nervous exhaustionist and modern invalid.*

LADY ANGELA, *a near-sighted lady and intimate friend of "The Beautiful N. E."*

MISS LUCY,
MISS JONES,
MISS SMITH,
And several others, } *acquaintances and relatives.*

AMELIA, *a delightful prude.*

HILDEGARDE, *a sympathizing maiden.*

CONSUELO, *called "The Countess."*

MISS EUNICE SMART, *a Church-woman.*

MR. WORTHINGTON, *a gentleman.*

LAWRENCE, *an observer.*

CYNICUS DOUCE, *a pessimist.*

And others.

ACT I., *Scene in a large city.*

ACT II., *Scene in "Paradise."*

TIME: *Late spring and summer vacation.*

COSTUME: *Present day.*

A FASHIONABLE SUFFERER.

ACT I.

Scene in a large city.   Time: Late Spring.

CHAPTER I.

A NEW SPECIES OF LUXURIOUS INVALIDISM.

HE salon, the dinner-table, and the club are not the only fields for the display of wit. Newer regions have been discovered which afford opportunity for its brilliant expression. Few of us naturally turn to the sick-chamber to find peculiar evidences of intellectual vigor, and yet to the sick-chamber must we go for just this very thing. Nowadays what

is called disease is not always treated with bitter
medicine and hot applications. A luxurious civilization has begotten a new order of invalids, who
exist on the sweet counsel of their physician and
the daily ministration of loving friends. The
house physician, like the house-fly, is in chronic
attendance upon them. Luckily, the modern medi-
cus is a charming fellow, and shows nothing but
velvet paws to his lovely patients. Harmless
" Apollinaris" and a half-grain of quinine are the
extent of his prescriptions. And while, to be sure,
his bill grows steadily larger and larger, yet his
pleasant and tidy appearance, punctually at eleven
o'clock, and the hope of final recovery constantly
held out, are worth twice the amount of his daily
fee. "Doctor, dear! come every morning, won't
you? I don't know what I should do unless my
monotonous day was relieved by your visit."

There is something terribly mysterious about
human nature. We are always stumbling upon it
in doing the simplest things. When going to bed,
or getting up, eating our daily food, or setting
about our daily task, this inscrutable mystery forces
itself upon us.

Among the many ways of its quixotic exhibition, there is none more queerly queer and un-
naturally natural than what is called " the nervous
exhaustion of ladies."

When one first hears of this affliction, he hesitates about approaching too near the unfortunate

victim who has "come down" with it. But he soon discovers it to be what the pretty school-girl said of love, — "an awful common complaint."

Although at first this disease appears to possess more of a physical than a metaphysical nature, still, when we consider that the fairer of the sexes is so wondrously constructed, — the intellectual and perhaps the celestial linked with the animal and the material, — the quizzical and the whimsical with the quibble-cal and the McFlimsey-cal, — constituting a bewildering hodge-podge of charms and other things, — it does not surprise us to detect, among these wonders, one of a metaphysical nature. Whatever be the truth, it is certain that the disease under discussion is a deceitful complaint. It generally attacks the handsomest and the richest of the sex, and seldom leaves them until all their friends die of it, for they themselves never do. It does not affect any particular vital organ, but flies about among them all, giving a little twist and pull to each, seriatim. First comes a sharp, wee quirk in the head, then a horrid neuralgic tweak in the "small" of the back ; and then again it "jangles" up and down the spine with agonizing force. But it somehow eases away again when the men of the family have gotten comfortably away to the "office," and a fresh log has been lighted on the tiled hearth, and the little chintz-lounge has been wheeled up close to the tall, bright andirons.

It is undeniable that there is a goodly number

of charming women in the world. — so many that

they may be said to form a class by themselves,

— whose vocation in life, an ill-natured person
might say, is to trade upon their supposed weaknesses with the rest of the world. Really nervous,
lacking bodily vigor, and at first requiring both the
sympathy and the attention of their friends, they
end by becoming beautiful tyrants, before whom
everybody must make obeisance. Taking advantage of their chronic exhaustion, they traffic upon
their allowed infirmities with consummate skill.
they have headache every morning regularly.
They generally lie a-bed until noon : have their
breakfasts brought to them as they recline with
languid grace upon big frilled pillows : a wren's
leg on toast, perhaps, a bit of a chop *en papillote*,
a snip of a roll, with a tiny pat of the yellowest
butter, are sufficient for them to taste of and send
away again. Before a genial wood-fire they deck
and dawdle with powder-puff and Lubin : then repose, like sunlight, on the softest couch. Their
active minds devour at a glance the latest novel,
as they are forbidden by their doctor to do the
least work on account of their eyes. They are just
well enough to go to the opera and the play : just
sick enough *not* to go to church. They sit up past
midnight in the easiest of chairs, at whist or something worse : then make the whole house go on tiptoe the next morning on account of the "agony"
in their heads.

They are very pretty, and have something about
them so delightfully fragile, like Sèvres or Dres-

den ware, that one is always desiring to touch
them, but is ever afraid to do so, lest something
might "come off," and they die on one's hands.
Sad to relate, these charmers are the veriest hum-
bugs in the world. Some people have fits, and we
pity them. Others have chronic distortions, and
we "thank our stars" that we have escaped that
sort of martyrdom; but to be a "Nervous Exhaustionist" — which is about the same thing nowadays
as saying that one is rich and fashionable — is getting to be rather an envied and enviable lot in life.
Of all the lovely and becoming diseases this is the
most accommodating, for it permits its victims to
sit for three hours on the hardest seats to hear
"Patience," or witness a ball-match, while it for-
bids them, for fear of a relapse, either to take a
needle in their jeweled hands, or tie a ribbon of
one of their children's bonnets. A single consider-
ation only prevents us from saying that one good
honest woman in the house who says what she
means, and means what she says, is worth a bag-
ful of this other kind. But there is *one* consider-
ation which stops us, and that is, that among this
female invalid-corps are found some of the loveliest
of the sex. They are fascinating to a degree that
is surprising, in view of their weak backs, and so
languidly lovable that it gets to be a privilege at
last to pay their doctors' bills, and be scolded by
their soft, sweet voices. One beautiful blonde
"exhaustionist" in a family keeps everything and

everybody lively. The children are glad to have one because of the tidbits of fruit and jelly which they purloin from the invalid fund. The men of the house are pleased because they meet so many "nice people" up in "dear Madeleine's bower."

There is a subdued fragrance of rose-buds and lemon-verbena always lurking about one of these secluded grottos. "Dear Madeleine" gracefully rests on the rich crétonne sofa, in a rose-pink *peignoir* cut polonaise. Her coiffure is of the latest and most charming mode. The color of her hair is a softish, childish, goldenish brown, with delicate "exhaustion" undulations all over it. Great grayish-blue eyes roll about between their dark, moist fringes; and when, from sheer exhaustion, they rest themselves upon yours, they have an enervating sort of an effect upon you, and you commence to experience the first sweet symptoms of nervous exhaustion creeping over your senses. A flash on the cheek, caused by your too sudden entrance, is still visible while the pink, taper fingers dally among the leaves of the last romance with exhaustive elegance.

Talk about the confining effect of sick rooms! I would much rather soothe the graceful contortions of a "Nervous Exhaustionist," than administer to the wants of any other patient in the world. Then again, the conversations to be heard in the boudoirs of this peculiar sect are often of the most delightful and racy character. An intelligent, quick-

witted specimen will amuse her friends for the hour
together. To be convinced that the graceful art of
conversation still thrives, it is only necessary to
enter within the scented precincts of one of these
nervous centres.

CHAPTER II.

A Scene within the Salon of an N. E.

FACTS NECESSARY FOR THE BETTER UNDERSTANDING OF THIS CHAPTER.

PERSONS INTRODUCED.

The Beautiful N. E. ; Mr. Cynicus Douce.

HE Beautiful N. E. is a lady of thirty-five, possessing comeliness both of face and person. She is bright, intelligent, and gray-eyed : gifted also with the womanly art of coquetry in the most finished style. Several years ago she married one of the twenty lovers who sought her hand, and became a widow after a short campaign on the doubtful field of matrimony. Her husband left her his fortune, which

was an ample one. Naturally given to luxuriou
living, she imperceptibly surrendered herself to it
blandishments, until she became a dependent an
almost helpless being. She is both lovely and lov
able, and these very traits have gradually seduce
her into a detestable dilettanteism which threaten
to spoil her character. She knows society by heart
and she lies on her downy couch, just sipping –
like a graceful sybarite as she is — the cream
foam of life's fascinations. She allows the world t
"gang its own gait." provided it furnishes her wit
what she craves of its pleasures. She has becom
weakly, hypocondriacal, and *exigeante*. She ha
summoned a handsome physician to attend her, an
lives in a sort of medical bondage. She imagine
herself to be the most unfortunate of mortals, eve
while munching away at royal dainties, and is eve
comparing her dreadful lot with that of her friend
who are so fortunate as to possess good digestion
but no money.

She has known Cynicus Douce from childhood
They have "summered and wintered" each othe
through many vicissitudes. They have quarrelec
and fought out all their youthful grievances, anc
have reached a point at last where solid friendshij
has survived all other feelings. The N. E.'s mothe
and Mr. Douce's father were at one time associatec
together in a very important and tender relation
which exhibited itself in an intimacy between thei
children. The Beautiful N. E. is a gorgeous crea

ture, though living under a tissue of fancied ailments. She resembles a magnificent jewel which has received a coating of some base medium which clouds its brilliancy.

Mr. Cynicus Douce is a gentleman forty years of age, is well-born, well-educated, and decent-looking. His father's father was named Theophilus, and fought in the Revolutionary War. His mother's father was half-brother to one of the signers of the Declaration of Independence (which made his family respectable). He graduated from Harvard College. He has had sisters, but they are dead. He is worth eighty thousand dollars in United States bonds. He is generous, quick-tempered, warmhearted, and blonde. Mr. Douce has large experience in what is called "society"; is considered, by his friends, as an oldish bachelor, who might, under certain provoking circumstances, marry somebody. He loves children and dogs, and *has* loved women. Society pets him, because he rather amuses society. He holds positive views on the current topics of the day, and sometimes expresses them. He is a gentleman devoid of "stuff or nonsense;" and his pet hobby through life is — hatred of shams.

The scene of this chapter is laid in a chamberparlor of a mansion fronting south, in one of our principal cities.

Sun shining most of the day in front windows; soft moquette carpet on floor; luxurious Persian rugs spread about; commodious fire-place, heavily

tiled; brass. antique andirons and fender: cherry
wainscot. five feet high. running round the room
cherry-wood mantel. covered with placques and
wonderful specimens of china: oval mirror above
mantel-piece. with dragons and crystal danglers
long. graceful lounge wheeled up to wood-fire
small clover-shaped table set with silver *tête-à-tête*
service: roses and violets in pretty vases: books
and magazines in profusion everywhere: a dish o
rare fruit on a little buffet at side: elaborate lace
curtains about windows: pink. down-lined slippers
at foot of lounge: small Skye-terrier rolled up
asleep. on cushion: two of Harmon's pictures on
rose-tinted walls: six phials. a silver spoon. half
tumbler of water. and ivory prayer-book on side
table: piece of half-finished pongee on arm o
lounge: the Beautiful N. E.. arrayed in becoming
morning attire. discovered reclining with soft Chud
dah shawl on her lap. reading a book just received
from the booksellers. (She shakes her pretty head
from time to time as she reads.)

(Enter servant.) *Ser.* "Mr. Douce is below
madam. and asks if he can see you."

Beautiful N. E. "Tell him to come up. Mary."

Ser. "Yes. madam." (Exit.)

(Enter Mr. Douce. hat in hand. with a smile on
his lips, and a piece of lemon-verbena in his button
hole.)

N. E. "How do you do. my friend? I'm glad
to see you, if for no other reason than to get your

opinion on something I have just received from the publishers. It is evidently written by an unmarried cynic."

"Male or female?" asked Mr. Douce, as he seats himself in an arm-chair.

"A cynic is always a *male!*" replied the N. E.

"Why an unmarried one, then?"

"Because his spunk shows he's not yet come to the altar."

"The halter, or the altar, did you say?" said Mr. Douce.

"You'll find them to be one and the same thing, my friend, whenever you get bold enough to approach in their neighborhood."

Cyn. "You seem strong enough to read this *something* to me?"

"I will, and willingly, too," she answered. "There's no name to the work. It simply has an interrogation point for a title" —

Cyn. "That fact, then, makes it *questionable*, I should say."

"I'll guarantee, though, it won't hurt *your* morals. Listen! The first chapter is entitled, 'Animated Female Molecules — their Structure and Habits.'"

"That certainly sounds like a woman-hater of the most venomous kind," said Douce.

"Wait till you hear it," said the beautiful sufferer, as her pink and diamondy fingers spread out on her lap the important document.

"Let me get that cushion to put just under your shoulders!"

"Thanks!"

Cyn. "And this little bench for your feet, perhaps?"

N. E. "Yes, I think so: but please remove those violets; they are too strong this morning!" Cynicus carried the violets to the other end of the room.

Cyn. "There! Will that do?"

N. E. "I'll trouble you just once more."

Cyn. "Certainly; what is it?"

N. E. " My vinaigrette. please." (Removing stopple and taking a sniff.) " Bliss! I'm all arranged now: but don't you even cough while I'm reading. I can't bear interruptions!"

" I'll hold in till the last minute." said Mr. Douce.

The Beautiful N. E. then read in sweet tones

THE PAPER OF THE UNMARRIED CYNIC.

" The machinery which goes to make up what is called 'Woman' is said to be very intricate. Philosophers assert that so complex a work could never have been achieved by finite power. Subtler and more æsthetic material was required to develop this mysterious creature than was needed to construct the more ordinary mortal. These scholars tell us that when this weird and incongruous thing issued forth from the Almighty's alembic in all the glory of her perfection. she was as much a riddle to herself as she was to the worshiping universe which received her. And in this particular. philosophy must be correct.

" This beautiful and apparently harmless creature. with her velvety skin. and her child-like demeanor, is not. however. to be trusted to that limitless extent to which, at first sight. uninitiated youth is ready to accord to it. And the inexperienced mortal who pins his faith. or bets his last dollar on that child-like innocence. that innocuous lambkinity will sooner or later discover his mistake. The unsophisticated youth will find that the pretty red blaze of the fire will burn his hands if he incautiously tries to clutch it. These same philosophers go on to say that, superadded to the mental and physical qualities which a woman has in common with man, she possesses a nicer discrimination, a subtler perception than he ever dreamed of. These great qualities give her immense advantages over her natural enemy. Some of her every-day qualities, such as secretiveness, passion, jealousy, vanity, ambition, self-control, and intrigue, become both dangerous and irresistible when wielded by a character possessing the combined attractions of a Venus and a Minerva. Such an one can crush without mercy, slay without quarter, pursue with unflagging energy, and stoop to the meanest subterfuges to attain her desire. A merciful Providence has taken pity upon the other half of humanity, however, and so arranged it that the heart and moral affections should be woman's great governing principle. So that, luckily for man, these more insubordinate elements of her disposition are thus kept in healthy subjection; and it results that as these different impulses gain or lose ascendency over her heart and affections, woman becomes either a good, docile, domestic creature; a dutiful wife and a model mother; a woman of the world, a flirt, a reformer, a criminal, or a nun."

(Here the Beautiful N. E. ejaculated, "All this is perfectly absurd!" and then proceeded.)

" Among the multifarious circumstances to which woman is called upon to adapt herself, there are none in which her natural powers come more readily into play than in her association with man. In the arena of society she is a curious and interesting study, and astonishes a student of her character with constant surprises. Self-poised and alert; ' uncertain, coy, and hard to please;' eternally on guard, vigilant as an outpost ; 'dying' to give the ' *coup de grâce*,' she prowls about her antagonist and wearies him out by her mosquito-ments. Few women reach their teens without becoming conscious of their attractiveness to the other sex. A desire to exercise an influence over man springs into existence the moment this consciousness is felt. A woman then becomes possessed of two antagonistic and almost irresistible impulses : the one is to attract a man and compel his allegiance ; the other is to repel and torment her victim the moment her tactics succeed. That which the world calls ' snubbing ' is as much a department of woman's code of love as to capture her natural foe. Like the English Constitution, a good deal of this code is unwritten. Precedent and the exigencies of each particular case furnish the law of conduct. No successful and fascinating woman, however, would consider her work handsomely performed unless she had first seized upon her little mouse, and then had legitimately introduced to him the dying-by-inches method, in order to make him realize his own abject situation and her complete victory. When she starts upon the war-path, like a good general, she first instinctively hides away her own affections in the thickest covert; then she gayly marches forth to combat, with her bright stiletto in her hand, and with a *picture* of a heart on her banner. She meets a foe who comes lumbering up to the fight, bearing his heart on his sleeve, and with his face uncovered. Every day we see such couples descending into the 'Valley of Decision,' the one in light marching order, with slender rapier and agile step; the other with his sword in its scabbard, and his plan of attack displayed to the enemy, inviting destruction. What a woman loves most is to play upon the edge of danger, and dance dalliance with 'her dearest foe.' Without hesitation she gives battle against overwhelming odds, having a vague hope, also, that she may be taken prisoner, if only for the pleasure of fighting again for liberty. Yet, with all this apparent recklessness, she takes precious care to keep a wide road open for retreat, and flies back to her reserves the moment the enemy opens upon her with grape and canister.

"In some of these foolhardy skirmishes she falls a victim to her own temerity. But even then, her conqueror finds it the most difficult of his labors to discover the place where her affections, if she has any, are concealed. Once entrapped, however, she enters into the harness of life, either with the ethe-

real mildness of the lamb, to subside into the ordinary humdrum of matrimony ; or else like that ob-
durate animal whose mission seems to be to kick
in the traces, to take the bit in its mouth, and to
'run away' with somebody, perhaps not its owner."

When the languid sufferer finished reading, she
said, "Now, my friend, what do you think of all
that rubbish?"

"I think," remarked Cynicus, "it is worth
thinking of."

"I would like to know," said the Beautiful N.
E., "what a woman is to do when she meets a man
in society? Can she be blamed for concealing her
affections from every booby who comes along?"

"I did n't say," said Mr. Douce, "that she was n't
to do this."

"Well, then," said the N. E., with quite a peach-
bloom on her cheeks.

"And that," continued Cynicus, "is just what
this wretch says who wrote the paper."

"No matter if he does; there is running all
through it a vein of sarcasm which is perfectly irri-
tating; and as to wearing their hearts on their
sleeves, I never saw a man in my life who ever had
any to wear!"

"You must be speaking, my dear Madeleine, of
those dreadful creatures whom you used to meet
at the balls, before you were prostrated by disease.
What do you say of man in his fresh and youthful

state, untrammeled by the experiences of a season with all you knowing ones?"

"I know nothing of man in his fresh and youthful state," said the invalid. "Unsophisticated youth seldom passes under my ken. Such a sight would be a sensation indeed! But," she added, "do you think, my friend, that what this creature has written is true?" (eying him with searching scrutiny).

"Suppose I said I did n't think it was?"

"Then, from my womanly perception, you would say what I *know* you did n't think!" Here the N. E. pushed her wavy hair back from her lily forehead.

Cyn. "If that is so, you 've answered the question for me; besides, the subject is too delicate a one to embrace at once."

N. E., laughing. "Nonsense! I 've seen you embrace twice as delicate a one, in much less time! Come, my friend, you *must* answer!"

"What is the alternative," asked Cynicus.

"Death!" said the Beautiful N. E., with mock gravity.

"Then I'll answer you as the Yankee did 'Jemima's' mother, who accused him of kissing her daughter half a dozen times behind the door. He replied, 'It's sort o' true, and sort o' not true, marm, for I only swapped five of mine for one she g'in me.'" (Exit Cynicus, who rises and escapes.)

"Good-morning!" (The Beautiful N. E. shakes her pretty forefinger at him as he closes the door.)

CHAPTER III.

Another scene within the same vale of misery as preceding chapter, containing a discussion of a certain kind of poetry.

DESCRIPTION OF CHARACTERS NOT BEFORE INTRODUCED.

THE Lady Angela. This friend of the Beautiful N. E. is about the same age as the invalid, and is gifted with many attractions of mind and body. Her eyes are of a true violet color, though not large. These, together with a profusion of dark brown hair, make her handsome. Her near-sightedness interferes somewhat with directness of expression. She is clever, brimful of vivacity, and

possessed of self-reliance and great administrative
talent. Truthful, open-handed, and charitable to a
fault, she has few emotions, a limited amount of
sentiment, and no "gush" whatever. Little given
to joking, and utterly unsuspicious, she treats all
the events of life seriously, yet she is like a child
in her appreciation of the delights and the merriment of life, and is the great power in the society
in which she moves, — carrying to a successful issue everything she undertakes. Always reliable,
and never weak, she is a charming mixture of self-
will and brilliancy, intelligence and audacity, innocence and resignation. Her wilfulness and decision
of character sometimes make her unjust, yet she is
so healthy in tone and so vigorous in action that
nothing can resist her progress. The Lady Angela
is a great friend of Mr. Cynicus Douce, and is constantly to be seen, in company with him, in the
apartment of her friend, the "Nervous Exhaustionist."

*Scene in Mr. Douce's apartment. Enter Servant, bringing
note, which Mr. Douce takes and opens.*

"*Tuesday, April 5th.*

"DEAR CYNICUS, — Come round this morning
and fetch your little paper on modern poetry. I
wish to be amused, and my whim to-day is, that
you are just the man to fill up the blank between
my woman-rubber and luncheon. Come by eleven.

"Yours in great pain. MADELEINE."

3

On receiving this note Mr. Douce twirled his moustache, donned a becoming cravat, his checked trousers, and a very benignant expression of counte-

nance, and, in obedience to the summons, hastened, with the desired paper under his arm, to the home of his friend, the N. E. The door-bell was answered by Thomas, a tall, thin-necked house-servant, very pale and very constant, and with a quiet, unnervous voice — most appropriate for an invalid's attendant. The visitor flitted like a burglar, up the easy flight of stairs, and landed at the top of it on an Aubusson carpet and *vis-a-vis* with the tidiest of ladies' maids. She smilingly opened the door, from which the odor of freshly cut flowers stole forth, and he crossed the threshold with becoming composure. As Mr. Douce looked about the elegant apartment and observed the almost innumerable objects of luxury which lay in heaps on every side, he murmured to himself, "Who wouldn't be a nervous exhaustionist? How delicious to be combed and brushed by that pretty lady's-maid, and then laid away to dry before that charming fire! To be fed with crumpets and jelly from morning till night, and rubbed and fondled like a boy's moustache! To lie in state on such a mountain of frills, and be decked with flowers, and sprinkled with such delicious odors! And then, there are the grapes, and the 'rubber,' and the sympathy, and the hairdresser! Ah, me! I should certainly get sick in spite of myself, with all these advantages."

Mr. Douce murmured this to himself as he removed his gloves, and endeavored to adapt his ignoble lungs to the soft, tropical atmosphere of this haunt of agony. The Lady Angela was sitting with "dear Madeleine," so it was not long before they all

three got into a pleasant conversation. As was natural, a variety of topics were touched upon, — pol-
itics, fashion, and the last bit of what they all had
"heard." Lady Angela's eyes were very blue, and
her hair was very brown; and although she was
near-sighted, her mind was in a most healthy condition, and needed no binocular telescope to see
what was in front of it. And then the fresh, breezy
way in which she expressed her opinions was a treat
to hear. She had all the frankness of a girl, with
the experience of a pretty woman. This mixture
of brains and elasticity made her exceptionally
agreeable.

"You're a fine, obedient fellow," said the Beautiful N. E., addressing Mr. Douce; "for I see
you've brought your 'paper' with you."

"Yes," said Cynicus, "like a deposit in the bank,
I'm kept 'on call.'"

"I'm much complimented, notwithstanding, that
you honored my draft so quickly," said the N. E.
with a twinkle in her eye.

"Ah! my dear Madeleine! I answer all your
notes at sight," gallantly replied Mr. Douce.

"Have your notes never gone to protest, Mr.
Cynicus?" gayly interposed Lady Angela.

"None, I trust, *you* ever indorsed."

"That's perhaps because I allow more than the
usual grace!"

"You can well afford to do that out of your abundance."

"My credit, however, is all gone to-day!" remarked Lady Angela.

"Why, where has it gone?"

"In the words of the immortal Mantalini, 'To the demnition bow-wows,' for I've been buying a dog."

Cyn. "One of those idiotic pugs, I see! But pugs don't pay, Lady Angela."

Lady A. "That's why I've got to pay *for* him." (She smiled at her own facetiousness.)

Cyn. "Still, you made by the operation, for now you've two: the one in your lap, and the other on the back of your head, madam."

Lady A. "Don't insult my scanty back-hair with your poor jokes, if you please!"

Cyn. (Laughing.) "Pray, excuse me. I'll drop it at once. It's so small a matter."

The Beautiful N. E. "Stop your sauciness, cousin Cynicus, and tell us if you have read Trollope's 'Dr. Wortle's School,' and what you think of it."

Cyn. "One of the most interesting stories I ever read. Dr. Wortle was a grand old fellow, wasn't he?"

Lady A. "Indeed he was: but how do you regard the conduct of Mr. and Mrs. Peacocke?"

N. E. "I pitied them from the bottom of my heart."

Lady A. "Yes, and so did I; but they did very wrong all the same!"

"I'd like to know what else they could have done to remedy the trouble, that they didn't do?" asked Cynicus.

"A good many things," replied Lady Angela.

"I'm sure they suffered enough for a concatenation of circumstances which *they* never brought about," said Cynicus.

"Yes, they did bring it about," answered Angela.

Cyn. "Why, just as soon as Mr. Peacock ascertained what Robert Lefroy asserted concerning his brother, he —

"He did *what?*" asked Lady Angela.

Cyn. "He took measures to discover if this assertion was a fact."

"That was all well enough, but the trouble lay farther back than that," remarked Lady Angela.

Cyn. "Oh! Now don't tell me that he ought to have gone before the world and repudiated his wife, for I won't agree with you."

"What he ought to have done," said Lady Angela, slowly, "was to have gotten his wife divorced from Lefroy in America, and before they came to England."

Cyn. "How could he? His wife was all alone in the world; had no place to go to, no spot to live in; so he had a right, I think, to shield her from a horrible position, into which, through no fault of her own, she suddenly found herself.

Lady A. "Ah! no matter. He should have left

her and procured this divorce. They could have
loved each other just the same, and lived apart!"

"I suppose that, on the strictest moral ground,"
said the Beautiful N. E., with a flush on her handsome face at the bare thought of the dreadful situation in which Mr. and Mrs. Peacocke were placed,
— "I suppose that, on the strictest moral grounds,
they should have stopped just where they were."

"Where *were* they? I'd like to know," said
Cynicus. "The mischief was done. They were
married, and Mr. Peacocke was too much of a Christian to have left his wife in some boarding-house,
with no money and no friends, to the tender mercies
of her own sex, — a treatment from which, as an
innocent woman, she must have died."

Lady A. "Why couldn't he have procured this
divorce, I repeat?"

Cyn. "I suppose you think, Lady Angela, that
a fellow can get 'unspliced' as easily as they say
he can out West in Indiana, where the train stops,
and the conductor announces at the door, 'Fifteen
minutes for divorce"; but it is a more difficult job
than that, I can tell you."

"Difficult or easy," said Lady Angela. "I know
perfectly well what Mr. Peacocke *ought* to have
done; but if he had done so, Trollope couldn't have
told us his story, you know."

"And I know," said Cynicus, "if I had been
Dr. Wortle, I would have done just what that splendid old fellow did ; and if I had been Mr. Peacocke,

with such an angel for a wife as Mrs. Peacocke,
I'd — well, I would have 'hung to her' forever."

"That's pretty well said for a bachelor," remarked the Beautiful N. E. "But 'Dr. Wortle's
School' has put out of our heads the little paper on
poetry which our friend was about to read to us.
Go on, Douce, I'm crazy to disagree with you."

As the "Nervous Exhaustionist" said this, she
crossed her tiny blue-silk-stockinged feet, and settled herself to listen, while Mr. Cynicus Douce ka-
hemmed once or twice, and then began his essay on

"SOME FORMS OF MODERN POETRY.

"It is impossible for language to describe our
highest thoughts or purest joys. The very process
of putting them into words cheapens them to me-
diocrity. Thoughts and emotions which are supremest must ever remain unutterable. They can
at best be suggested by glance of eye or tone of
voice. They are murdered in attempted articula-
tion. Notwithstanding this, man is ever trying to
syllable the unutterable, and poetry is the chosen
medium for this attempted expression. The world
acknowledges that, as one of the fine arts, none of
her sisters holds a prouder position.

"A poetic mind is made out of finer clay than
other kinds. Homer, Virgil and Horace, Milton,
Shakespeare and Dante, Scott, Byron and Words-
worth, with *id omne genus*, were all poets indeed.
Their names and their works need but be men-

tioned to be extolled. To be called a poet is a different thing, however, from actually being a poet. There are shoals of creatures who dream that they dwell on Mount Parnassus, when they mistake the bottom for the top of it. There is a certain form of modern poetry which is pure bosh. It misleads instead of instructing anybody, it degrades instead of elevating one's soul, and it is as inappropriate to the needs of the age as a high-necked apron would be to the wants of a Zulu. If grand-sounding words, describing disembodied phantoms clutching after the unutterable, be poetry, then we have lots of it.

"To some minds, the divine art is mere sound; like the monotonous droning of summer bees, or the flowing of water over a dam. It makes but little difference to them that no sense is conveyed; for so long as the poet's object is sufficiently obscured, and the rhythm and the feet are all there, and other folks who can't understand it are envying them who can, although even *they* can't,—why, that is poetry.

"I am unable to fathom a good deal of this sort of modern rhyme, chiefly because I fail to discover, at a glance, the governing verb of the long sentences. It does n't seem to come in at the proper place; so in looking for this verb I lose all the sentiment of the lines. Then again, the jingle and the rhythm 'get away' with me, leaving my comprehension far in the rear. It is a nuisance to be

so constantly obliged to stop in order to allow one's
mind to 'catch up.' Then I never know just who
is talking,—whether Sir Roland de Graeme said
all that about 'the eagle's scream on rocky crag,'
or the Lady Gwendolyne. Again, when I have at
last decided that the knight was certainly the party

> ' Whose cheek was blenched with ashen hue '

at what the Lady Gwendolyne told him, I am hope-
lessly involved by this line, which follows immediately after,—

> ' At this relation *she* turned pale.'

So I am forced to go 'way back again to where
'moonlight mists lie on the moat,' and with forefinger retrace carefully, line by line, until I reach
the place where I was brought to a stand. Now,
this way of enjoying poetry is nonsensical; and I
think I must be made up differently from the rest
of the world to find this æsthetic occupation such
a difficult task."

"Yes, you must be," interrupted the Beautiful
N. E., "for this rhythmic cadence is fascinating to
me. The *sense* is not everything in a poem, my
friend: you are altogether too prosaic."

"No matter," said Lady Angela, laughing.
"Let's agree that he *is* made of different stuff
from other people; and what is more, that there
is neither rhyme nor reason about him."

"Why, haven't I the required number of feet
for a poet?" said Cynicus, laughing.

"I suppose so, Cynny, for both of yours are spondees," replied Lady Angela, fairly blushing at the horrible joke she had perpetrated.

N. E. (In great merriment, and smelling a nosegay.) "Go on, my friend: we beg your Grace's pardon for interrupting all your eloquence."

"I envy those young ladies," continued Mr. Douce, "who sit together under the elm-trees, and read for hours 'Locksley Hall' and Mrs. Browning and Mr. Browning, and understand so easily every word these authors say. And when they are devouring the seductive style of modern poetry under discussion, they go steadily on, galloping forward, verse after verse, — never looking back until the gloaming shuts out the printed page from their pretty eyes. Besides, they intuitively perceive the truthfulness of those wonderful revelations of the inner inwardness of Lady Gwendolyne's consciousness when she won the knight, and the naturalness of her 'buoyancy anent her wrongs;' which, I, somehow, cannot fathom, and so consequently envy them.

"They never stop, unless to draw breath or 'turn over.' They know just what *he* did, and just what *she* did, and just what they *both* did, and what became of it all.

"'No trouble,' say they, 'all perfectly clear,' 'perfectly lovely,' 'so musical,' 'so rhythmical,'—

> "'That haughty knight of de Lorraine,
> Like mists athwart the roaring main,
> . . . Clutched at her jeweled, silken train;
> He bore aloft 'mid blood and pain,
> 'T were better that he ne'er had ta'en,
> O Gwendolyne! thy gentle rein!—
>
> .   .   .   .
>
> He spoke but once, then closed his eyes;—
> The palfrey gray—and bridle-wise!—
> 'Ah me!' he said. 'O Paradise!'—

Oh! It's just splendid!"

"Ah! now you are speaking of those mawkish school-girls, who are hardly out of pantalets," said the N. E.

"No! not altogether of that kind," answered Mr. Douce. "The class I have reference to includes also girls whose feet, to be sure, are often seen below their dresses; but not because their gowns are not long enough."

"Because why, then?" said Lady Angela.

"Because their stockings are so pretty," replied Cynicus. "But why do you interrupt me so often: you will lose all the continuity."

Mr. Donce then resumed, —

"I make these remarks to inveigh against that unhealthy sentiment of the present day which indulges in senseless rhapsodies over mere rhythmic cadence.

"True poetry is emotion, and its office is to elevate humanity. Here the ideal comes legitimately into use, for when poetry deals in natural events, and describes the different phases of human thought and feeling, it is permitted to idealize these subjects. Just as the true artist, using his knowledge of the facts and attributes of nature, adds to all this his own ideal conception, without violating any recognized verity.

"The bosh-poetry of the present day does not follow any of these laws. It describes nothing but the unreal and the unnatural. It throws about itself such a veil of unintelligibility as to obscure the small figment of sense it may be supposed to contain. It depends for its effect upon high-sounding words, — a certain originality of expression which is attractive, — any amount of gush, which is cheap, coupled with a thinly veiled *double-entendre* which is disgusting. Give me, in preference to such pinchbeck varieties, 'Lucy had a little lamb!' or, 'Where are you going, my pretty maid?" I can appreciate these simple ditties. They kindle emotion, and suggest pleasanter trains of thought than, for instance, the following lines addressed to

"'AMOR.

"'O spirit unutterable! O force divine!
    Abridged athwart the animal and the higher life,
Coexistent with earth's commencement! — entwine
    Thyself — an immortal legacy — about my wife!

"'Her golden hair make sensuous with thy presence!
    Its gossamer web, like flowers of the yellow sun,
Dropping in golden rain on ivory shoulders, whence,
    The pure irradiance of her breaths, but half begun

"'In loving heart below, doth warm these golden tresses
    Like gentle summer rays on some southern flowered slope;
Clearing away all signs of the heart's distresses,
    And bidding in their places to blossom sweet flowret Hope.'"

"Let us now translate this poem into plain English. A nameless individual — who seems to be a married man — calls upon the spirit of Love, a hybrid of earth and heaven, to entwine itself about his wife like an immortal legacy. '*Immortal* legacies' may possibly *twine* themselves. Mortal ones, however, are generally too small to do that. They expend their powers in mourning-rings, and black-edged note-paper.

"The second verse is rather æsthetic. The palpitating husband goes on to hope that this spirit will get into his wife's hair and make it sensuous: into her 'pug,' her 'crêpés,' and her 'bang.' It

must go all through it, in spite of hair-pins and
'false fronts,' so he can perceive it. Then he
poetically compares it to yellow sunflowers dropping in golden rain upon her ivory shoulders, —
'falling' would have been better, but no matter,
and as being warmed up by the 'irradiance of half-
breaths.' Think of half-breaths puffing up from
your wife's heart with irradiance, and warming this
golden hair, which, of course, in that case, must
have been all over her face! Now, as a matter of
fact, half-breaths never come up with any irradiance at all. There is no illuminating power in a
breath, much less a half-breath. I wish a light
breath was the same thing as a lighted breath, for
then we might save all our gas-bills, and be filled
with delight at the same time.
There are three or four other
objections to the 'half-breaths'
of this poem; one of these is
that, instead of clearing away
the 'heart's distresses,' they
actually redouble them. Neither do these 'semi-brefs' make
the 'sweet flowret Hope' to
'blossom,' because if they did
it would be holding out false
blossoms to the patient, as on
pure mathematical principles a
person could live only half as long on half-breaths
as he could on whole ones.

" Besides all this, nobody ever does anything of the kind. It is all poetic, æsthetic, and dyspeptic nonsense. But the poem sounds 'mighty pretty.'

> " ' Its gossamer web, like flowers of the yellow sun,
>   Dropping in golden rain.'

" Oh, dear! Is n't it too mum-mum for anything!

" There is a ring, however, about true poetry which goes directly to the heart and stays there. Here is something delicious from Shelley's poem of

" JULIAN AND MADDALO.

> " ' Oh! how beautiful is sunset, when the glow
>   Of heaven descends upon a land like thee,
>   Thou paradise of exiles, Italy.
>   Thy mountains, seas, and vineyards, and the towers
>   Of cities they encircle! It was ours
>   To stand on thee, beholding it; and then,
>   Just where we had dismounted, the Count's men
>   Were waiting for us with the gondola.
>   As those who pause on some delightful way,
>   Though bent on pleasant pilgrimage, we stood
>   Looking upon the evening, and the flood
>   Which lay between the city and the shore,
>   Paved with the image of the sky. The hoar
>   And airy Alps, towards the north, appeared
>   Between the east and west; and half the sky
>   Was roofed with clouds of rich emblazonry,
>   Dark purple at the zenith, which still grew
>   Down the steep west into a wondrous hue,
>   Brighter than burning gold, even to the rent
>   Where the swift sun yet paused in his descent
>   Among the many-folded hills. They were
>   Those famous Euganean hills, which bear,

As seen from Lido through the harbor piles,
The likeness of a clump of peaked isles ;
And then, as if the earth and sea had been
Dissolved into one lake of fire, were seen
Those mountains towering, as from waves of flame,
Around the vaporous sun, from which there came
The inmost purple spirit of light, and made
Their very peaks transparent. " Ere it fade,"
Said my companion, " I will show you soon
A better station." So o'er the lagune
We glided, and from the funereal bark
I leaned, and saw the city, and could mark
How from their many isles, in evening gleam,
Its temples and its palaces did seem
Like fabrics of enchantment piled to heaven.
I was about to speak, when " We are even
Now at the point I meant," said Maddalo,
And bade the gondolieri cease to row.
" Look, Julian, on the west, and listen well,
If you hear not a deep and heavy bell."
I looked, and saw between us and the sun
A building on an island, such a one
As age to age might add, for uses vile, —
A windowless, deformed, and dreary pile ;
And on the top an open tower, where hung
A bell, which in the radiance swayed and swung —
We could just hear its coarse and iron toague :
The broad sun sank behind it, and it tolled
In strong and black relief. " What we behold
Shall be the mad-house and its belfry tower,"
Said Maddalo ; " and ever at this hour,
Those who cross the water hear that bell,
Which calls the maniacs, each one from his cell,
To vespers." '

" Now how perfectly intelligible this is ! How
beautifully expressed ! How elevating in character ! and, at the same time how it idealizes the

facts and verities of nature!"   Here Mr. Douce
"ka-hemmed" once or twice more, and then proceeded.

"Incessant reading of indifferent poetry will in-
jure character.   An individual reared in a poetic
atmosphere, where it is mixed up with his daily experiences, will gradually become affected by it.   If
this atmosphere happens to be a mawkish and false
one, it will show itself in his character.   Just as a
continual diet of unsubstantial food will tend to
form a less noble specimen of physical health than
where there is an abundance of good beef and ale.
On this principle a false and sickly character would
be the result of daily doses of what are called 'emo-
tional lines,' 'rhapsodies of soul,' intuitive long-
ings,' 'argosies from heaven,' and such like.

"In time, such bosh would turn a Christian into
a sexless nondescript.

"We should not only read the best poetry, but
something else besides.   Specialists of any sort,
scientific, artistic, or aesthetic, are likely to become
little else than enthusiasts : and enthusiasts are in
danger of becoming deranged people, and deranged
people, after a while, get crazy.   Nobody can think
intensely, continually, entirely on one subject, give
up his whole mind to it, without getting oblivious
to other important interests, and sooner or later becoming an abnormal creature.   One man believes
in a vegetable diet, so he eats nothing but vegeta-
bles, until at last he is but little more than an or

dinary carrot. So it is with all other crazes which afflict society. Everything in this world can be overdone, and we suffer from it. The same may be said of poetry. Let us read it as we sip maraschino, — in its proper place. A bit of history, a novel or two, a little of the best poetry, then a few hours of recreation, and so on, until we reach that perfected state of living which we never can reach — until we die.'

"Oh dear!" ejaculated Lady Angela, "you do take such a dreary view of this subject! Don't you know, my dear fellow, that allowance must be made for a certain amount of what we call humbug! Human nature demands it. It is like the chit-chat and tittle-tattle of society, which serve to take the strain off the mind, which might otherwise break down under a continued pressure of the prosaic."

"Yes!" echoed the N. E. "Cranks and deranged people seem to be a necessity in this world. They act as mosquitoes and May-bugs do in summer, and call off our attention from more serious matters; the mere act of crushing them eases our minds."

"Ladies, pardon my smiling. You talk as if you were both weighed down by an insupportable load of care and trouble; but, perhaps, you are right. This is only my view of it. It is delightful, however, to think you don't agree with me, for I hate the humdrum of perfect accord as heartily as you do. What I particularly dislike is being humbugged and not to know it; it's rather pleasant if you

have that knowledge. No matter," continued Mr.
Douce, "I've only a trifle more to read, and then
you can pitch into me to your heart's content."

"There is a sort of poetry, however, which delights everybody, and which not only moulds character but enables the most prosaic of us to listen to
it without weariness. This poetry can hardly be
described, for you catch its mystic eloquence in the
turn of a wrist and in the pose of a head, in the
silver tone of laughter or on the crest of an arch
expression. Whole cantos can be acquired by
heart in the smallest moment of time, and volumes
'committed' before one can say 'Jack Robinson.'
Give me that kind of poetry —for it makes but
little difference whether 'love' rhymes with 'dove,'
or 'dart' with 'heart.' There is a deeper rhythm,
intelligible, unutterable, —which tells its story in
letters of light, either to the tyro of eighteen or the
veteran of fifty."

Silence reigned within the scented precincts of
the invalid's boudoir for the space of two full minutes; but was finally broken by our fair friend herself, who slowly remarked, —
"Now there is something true in what you say
about a certain style of modern poetry, yet you
can't make me hate it. 'Æsthetic mooning,' if you
will, but in spite of it all, the whole idea is so different from this everlasting talk about the 'Cen-

sus Bill' and the 'Chinese Question,' or whether
women will probably vote next summer, or what
will be the political significance of the removal of
some little postmaster in South Framingham, that
I hail a touch of this 'hifalutin' as a breath from
another sphere."

"You are more than half right, dear Madeleine,"
replied Lady Angela; "for even twaddle and nonsense have their proper places, and nothing is more
comforting, when one feels just like it, than to read
the most ecstatic and improbable romance, and to
gloat over the details of the most fiendish crimes."

"This sounds well, I must confess," said Cynicus
Douce, "coming from a woman who cries over an
old love-letter, and gives her last penny to help any
worthless tramp who passes her door."

"Never mind!" replied honest Lady Angela.
"We are all bundles of incongruities; and the
truth of the matter is that people are a good deal
better, and a good deal worse, than other people
think they are."

The Nervous Exhaustionist here grew a little
pale, but gracefully leaned over and took from the
table at her side a mysterious paper box, and said
in the softest accents: —

"Before you go, you must both taste the Countess Toots' wedding-cake. It was left at the Lega-
tion after the ceremony, and the Secretary sent it
over to me in the dispatch-bag: — just a crumb,
my friends, you know, to dream on!'"

"Oh! a crumb of *that* stuff looks black enough for the dream of death," answered Mr. Douce.

"Not if you took quinine, as I do, before eating. Would you mind passing the pellets?" said the Beautiful N. E.

"Not the least in the world. How many will 'settle' plum-cake?" inquired Douce.

N. E. "Now don't be foolish, Cynicus. My doctor prescribes one before each meal, and two before anything particularly indigestible."

Cyn. "Your doctor must be a surgeon, then."

N. E. "Why, pray?"

Cyn. "Because he's evidently preparing you for some horrid operation."

N. E. "Oh, you can't frighten me: he lets me eat everything. He says where nervous prostration has taken place, patients are to have their own will."

"I wish my nervous centre was prostrated, then," said Mr. Douce.

"You're incorrigible," said Lady Angela. "But we *must* go now, Madeleine, dear; don't exert yourself too much, for it will be sure to put you back just where you were last fall."

N. E. "Exert myself! It's impossible, I can assure you. I just lie here all day, thinking over what I'd like to do if I were only as well as both of you. I tired myself all out this morning trying to decide whether I would better trim my 'white albatross' with 'Spanish blonde' or 'Languedoc.'"

Lady A. "Ah! you must be careful, Madeleine; don't do too much; that's your trouble, dear; good-by."

"Good-by," said the Beautiful N. E., plaintively, as the door closed upon her two friends.

"My dear Cynicus," said Lady Angela, when they were both on the street, "what *do* you think is the matter with Madeleine; has she any *real* disease?"

"Whatever she has, I could cure her in an hour," said Mr. Douce.

Lady A. "How, I should like to know?"

Cyn. "Tell her to *do* something."

Lady A. "She's a splendid creature!"

Cyn. "Yes, she *is* a splendid creature, dying of manition."

Lady A. "Well! dying of inanition is doing something, is n't it?"

Cyn. "Yes, beautiful woman, it is: but inanition, being merely action begun, demands too much exertion for her to ever finish; and that's the whole trouble with this peculiar class. They are always *going* 'to do something.'"

Lady A. "Ah, Cynicus, you are too hard on our friend; but seriously, let's do what we can to get her out of this miserable condition," said Lady Angela.

"I 'll do everything that 's proper," replied Mr. Douce, with mock seriousness.

CHAPTER IV.

AN INTERMEDIATE OR PURGATORIAL CHAPTER ALLOWED
FOR TRANSMIGRATION OF SOULS TO " PARADISE."

AFTER the first day of July city life becomes intolerable. Thirsty, heated, and kiln-dried humanity hankers for " green fields and pastures new." The idea of eventually going to Paradise is a cherished one in every heart. It is called " home " by many people ; and what term is fraught with more tender emotions ! There are, however, many little paradises which lie scattered about life's highway, which will do very well for the summer months.

and which convert the sorrows of exhausted nature
into temporary bliss. Scented clover and Alderney
cows, brown roads and quantities of cream, soft
beds, and lots of money, are good, solid, earthly
substitutes for the real paradisiacal article. They
certainly do effect a marvelous restoration of both
mental and physical powers; and at the same
time they are, perhaps, better suited to the present
groveling and sinful condition of man than the
other one would be.

Green peas and asparagus are delicious vegeta-
bles, but when coupled with the consciousness of
their being grown in one's own garden, they taste
even better than when eaten from the inimitable
cuisine of Delmonico.

There is a feeling of pride, equal to that of a
Roman emperor, when one can sit back in his
chair, at his own table, and say: " Try these peas,
they are the ' Early Favorite.' My gardener has a
secret of ' forcing ' which enables us to have them
on our table ten days before any of our neighbors.
Take some more, we have oceans of them." Even
though it is not " good form " to dilate on the merits of one's own larder, still, somehow, it will
" come out " before dinner is over. There inevitably comes an overweening temptation which cannot be withstood by an ordinary owner of a villa, to
remark off-hand, and incidentally of course, about
the " mutton," or the " gosling," or the " cauli-
flower," or the something else, which was raised on

one's own plantation.   And why shouldn't we talk
about "these things," I'd like to know?   I consider that summer-time is given to those of us who
are fortunate enough to own kitchen-gardens and
cold graperies, Southdown mutton and green geese,
for the precise purpose of expressing ourselves
in just this seignorial manner.   It engenders in us
a healthy sort of diathesis which goes a long way
towards bringing back tone and fibre to our city-
jaded natures ; and also enables us to return to
gloomy brick walls and flashing electric light with
a fresh stock of endurance.   It fairly makes a city
man's nature expand to take a stroll some fine June
morning over the fresh, green hills and sit down
beneath the shadowy elms.   It opens the cockles of
his heart to listen to the countless songs of the
birds which are caroling above him ; and for the
moment " selling short " and other " lingo " are
meaningless expressions.

He finds, too, that he had no idea there *were* so
many birds in the world, and, as to that matter, so
many *bugs* either, which makes him forthwith
spring up from the grass, and shake out his white
handkerchief whereon he sat.   (City people, when
they sit down, always spread their white handkerchiefs on the grass, for fear of malaria, and examine their ears for spiders, &c.)

He walks rapidly back to his breakfast with a
healthy appetite and a renewed amount of vigor.

These trivialities are all-important to city people.

They "rehabilitate" their nerves, and are a deal more efficacious than all the tonics of the pharmacopœia; bringing roses to the cheeks when quinine and iron utterly fail.

To one of these earthly paradises above suggested, a thirsty, sun-scorched, and tired humanity incontinently flies with its trunks, its poodles, and its white-livered children.

ACT II.

Scene: "Paradise." Time: Summer Vacation.

CHAPTER I.

EVERY-DAY EXPERIENCES WITH GIRLS AND THINGS, CON-
TAINED IN THE DIARY OF AN UNFORTUNATE GENTLEMAN.

THIS is intended to be a pleasant scene among
the rolling hills of Tucit-Kennoc. The party gathered on the lawn of the popular host of Paradise is
a congenial one, and consists of the following persons not before introduced to the reader : --

Amelia, a prude. This lady is a handsome
blue-eyed blonde ; thoroughly delightful to know,
charming to think about, and forever to be de-
pended upon.

Consuelo, the Countess, is the "salt of the earth,"

embodying perfectly Sir Walter's line " when pain and anguish," etc.

Grace is a black-eyed, black-haired darling, just seventeen, — dear, dangerous, and dreamy.

Hildegarde is a winsome, sympathetic, golden-haired, Germanesque lassie, who will well repay the affection of the noble-hearted man who can win her.

Mrs. George Madison Taggart of Middletown, Conn., is a lady who has recently been added to the number of guests at "Hill-Top." She is a precise and discreet sort of person, who appears to think that the world ought to listen when she speaks. Her remarks are delivered in jerky epigrams.

Lucretia Davis is a little, sombre-dressed indi-vidual, with novelistic tendencies, whose name has been connected with a romantic affair in Hartford. She always speaks with emotion, as if every word distressed her.

Lawrence is a keen, old-fashioned observer, de-lighting in a good joke, cultivated, traveled, and altogether reliable; moreover, he is a friend of Mr. Douce.

This pleasant company was seated on the green grass, chatting, sewing, and laughing at what had transpired in the miniature world about them since they last settled the "affairs of the nation." These "affairs" were "adjusted" regularly every afternoon, only to break forth afresh into new complications on the next.

The long shadows of the pines were already perceptible on the lawn. Some of the fair boarders enjoyed their siestas; others lay in hammocks or reclined with easy grace on the short, green grass. A soft westerly breeze came soughing over from "hamlet-hill," while the long-billed humming-birds were tremblingly poised among the honeysuckles.

"Do you know, *he* is going to tell us something about his experiences with girls?" said sweet Amelia, the prude.

"Such a subject requires to be handled very gingerly, and I don't wish Grace to hear it," spoke up Consuelo, the Countess.

"And discreetly, too," added Hildegarde, "for you all remember what trouble came of just my telling about a little experience *I* had once?"

"No *honorable* man would ever impart to an indiscriminate audience what had transpired in his privileged intimacy with the gentler sex," said Mrs. George Madison Taggart from Middletown.

"And expect to hold his head up in decent society afterwards," murmured Lucretia Davis, the woman with a history.

"Oh, there he comes! Mr. Douce, you won't be allowed to impart these horrid revelations to any one but myself. These other ladies are too unsophisticated to bear them," spoke up dear Miss Brown.

"*We* never said so," murmured a dozen voices.

"Well, but I know your mothers are all very particular as to what you hear and read, so Mr. Douce shall tell me these revelations in all their wild license, and then I can make such emendations as I think proper."

"What revelations do you refer to?" said Cynicus Douce.

"Why, some of your love affairs!"

"Don't be afraid; I never thought of telling them."

"You said so this morning at the 'corner,'" exclaimed the blonde-haired Amelia.

"Not at all! You certainly misunderstood me then, for I spoke of reading a sort of diary, written by an unfortunate stranger, — supposed to be a great personage, I believe, — dead now; giving an account of some of his experiences in life."

"I'm rather disappointed," replied Amelia, "for I hoped to hear his confessions."

"What a pity," said Grace, "my curiosity would at last have been satisfied on some points."

But Grace was immediately "squelched" by Aunt Consuelo, who never was in love — but once.

"Ladies, you all mistake me," said Mr. Douce. "I thought it might amuse you, as we sat here under the shadow of Benjamin's pines, to read some portions of a curious MSS. found in a chamber of an unknown gentleman who sighed himself to death last winter in the fourth story of No. 149,763 Walnut Street, Philadelphia."

"Oh, you're joking! It's not really so, is it?" said Hildegarde.

"Yes: really so! They found him lying, dying of sighing, his head resting gracefully on his left arm, his curly hair threaded with silver."

"Caused by disappointment, probably," said Amelia.

"Yes! caused by disappointment and despair," said Mr. Douce.

"Poor boy!" — "Was he handsome — and penniless?" — "How he *must* have suffered!" — "Do you suppose he had a title?" — asked several voices.

"Ladies," replied Mr. D., "I know not the particulars; simply these facts: his body and this MSS. were found together. The pen, with the ink still wet upon it, had dropped from his nerveless grasp, and was discovered lying on the floor beside his almost lifeless remains. They buried him at 'Laurel Hill,' in a nameless grave, until his family (if he had one) could be informed of the event."

Ladies. "Did he leave no effects?"

"Ladies, he left nothing."

Ladies. "Why! he must have had" —

At this moment Cynicus Douce saw his fair friend, the X. E., slowly emerge from the new cottage, and approach the charming group assembled on the lawn.

By dint of the combined persuasions of her doctor and friends, "dear Madeleine" had consented

to try what good a month among the hills would accomplish for her weakened nervous system. Her maid, Thomas the quiet man-servant, her quinine, her props — her little hair pillow to stuff under her left ear, — and all the other petty paraphernalia of invalidism, had been hauled up from the station by instalments, and at last were safely lodged on the ground-floor of the new villa on the hill-top.

The N. E. said she was "miserable," but in spite of that declaration, to outsiders she appeared beautiful, while the two roses on her cheeks, and her red pouting lips, suggested anything but nervous exhaustion.

Having safely deposited the blushing invalid — with her cloud of lace and ribbon — in the new hammock, and assisted Lady Angela to alight from her "buckboard" and join the pleasant party, our friend Douce unfolded the unfortunate gentleman's MSS., while "Old Harry," the dog, flung himself at his feet in the cool grass, and the red squirrels stopped cracking the cones overhead, to listen.

THE STRANGER'S MSS.

"This is no history. I don't know what it is, and care less. I write merely to stop myself from this horrible sighing, for I'm dying of sighing, caused by continual disappointment — no matter what.

"The only way I get the least relief is by trying to divert my mind from that which is crushing it by writing down anything, everything that comes into my head — about my youth, my travels, my observations, my experiences. Nothing much — very like what happens to everybody else.

"But the mere act of jotting it down stops my sighing and my repining for the time; that's why I'm doing it. . . . How well I remember my first experience in life. It was early in September that the little girl in the gray pelisse sang for me —

' Over the far blue mountains.'

No angel tones were ever sweeter, no siren voice ever touched nearer a little boy's heart. But what *was* that perfume she used to have about her? verbena? patchouli? musk? peppermint? What was it? 'Oh,' orris! It was orris. The remembrance of that odor brings back with it a flood of delightful recollections. What a clean, upper drawer and fresh-linen aroma has orris! One immediately thinks of mountains of tidy collars and immaculate cuffs, and starched hem-stitched handkerchiefs.

"The little girl with the gray pelisse had all these: and when on calling nights I caught a whiff of this orris-perfume and a glimpse of all those other delicious things which came cantering down the front stairs to see me, my heart throbbed as if it would fly out of my jacket.

"The little girl with the gray pelisse was older than I was, and consequently possessed more of what I afterwards discovered people called '*a plumb*'

than her youthful lovers had. The boys would call
upon her in shoals; and it was a common sight to
see ten or twelve of them, arrayed in their best
clothes, ranged along in chairs in her drawing-
room, with eyes fixed upon their idol, and ready
to 'giggle' at the slightest suggestion. A boy's
idea of bliss is to laugh immoderately at nothing.
How daintily she would trip up to the long row of
her young admirers and offer to each one a seed-
cake, saying, '*Voulez-vous du gâteau?*' in such
siren tones as were perfectly irresistible. I used
to take my cooky with trembling hands, while
great drops of perspiration and love stood on my
forehead.

"And then, to this day, I don't know whether
that hair-bracelet she furtively gave me, tied with
pink ribbons, was really her own hair or her
maid's. I have a dark suspicion it grew on this
latter creature's head. Somebody told me it did,
—forgotten who, possibly a rival. But that dark
suspicion made it my sad and imperative duty to
snatch the loved though faded object from my wrist
and throw it, with all fury, behind the back-log.

"Was it hers or was it not? The question will
never be settled, and perhaps it is better that it
should remain a mystery.

"Ah, dear girl! I thank thee for the delights of
that first experience of boyhood! Each little chapter of it is graven on my heart. The plum-cake,
the little billets-doux hid away between the leaves

of the fourth book on the second shelf of the first
alcove, in the public library, as you enter; and
then the valentines! 'None know thee but to love
thee,' etc. Every one of these precious memories
is as vivid as if I had cried over them but yesterday. No king was prouder than I was in my little
realm of love. I dwelt of a truth in the 'happy
valley,' until one day a great elderly snubby man
broke into my elysium and stole thee away. Poor
unsuspicious boy that I was? Why, I did n't know,
dear girl, thou ever knew him, much more loved
him. And so all the while thou wert saying ' *Voulez-vous du gâteau*' in those dulcet tones, and wert
sending to thy boyish admirer thy maid's hair tied
with ribbons, instead of thine own, and wert indit-
ing to him lines of constancy; that great elderly
rival was 'making up' to thee with his insinuat-
ing smiles, which thou wert appropriating with
consummate, *spirituelle* grace, thus cheating thy
poor callow lover! Longfellow piped a solemn
verity, in more ways than one, when he sang, 'Tell
me not in mournful numbers — things are not what
they seem.' An eventful career, since those youthful days, has proven that not only little girls, but
big ones as well, are 'things' which 'are not what
they seem to be' at first, and before they know
you admire them."

After reading this brief but harmless episode,
every lady got up and sat down again on the other

foot, and asked each other some of those regular questions which usually accumulate after occasions of enforced female silence, such, for instance, as, "Is No. 90, or 100, the best cotton to mend cambric dresses with?" etc.

Mr. Douce complacently ate a peach pending this passing flurry, and after flinging the stone clear over the white fence into the road beyond, went on to the next chapter in the diary of the unfortunate stranger, which was entitled : —

"A CASE OF ROMAN FEVER.

"From Malta to Messina, thence to Naples, and so on to Rome, in time for the ceremonies of Holy Week, was only a pilgrimage of love. Every step of the way opened lovelier scenes to a mind already filled with beautiful reminiscences of Naples and the upper Nile. When Pius IX. first became Pope

the celebrations clustering about the Easter-tide
were gorgeously observed in the holy city, while
the Pontifical States were still an acknowledged
power among the nations of the earth. Besides,
a *dolce far niente* life in Egypt had created a zest
for more stirring scenes, and I hailed with especial
delight the dome of St. Peter's, which I caught
sight of from the diligence on the road from Porto
d'Ansio.

"It goes without saying, that Rome was full of
strangers, and I soon discovered many kind friends
whom I had met on my travels. I obtained, with
great difficulty, one half of an apartment in the
Via di Bocca Leone, from an obliging traveling companion, from whom I had but just parted at Malta,
and felt perfectly contented that I had been even
so fortunate as that. There is but one Rome in
the world, and life in the city in the 'good old
times' was somewhat different, I trow, from the
more modern *régime*. It was smaller than it is
now, and it resembled a delicious *pâté*, composed
of the choicest morsels, compressed together within
the smallest compass.

"There were some delightful English acquaintances living in the Via Condotti, whom I was fortunate enough to fall in with, and who insisted
upon my joining their party, and making, in their
company, the tour of the city. These lovely people — only two, George Melville and his wife Griselda — were just young enough to appreciate

everything. They had money, health, and no children, so they floated about among the wonders of the world, leading a most fascinating existence.

"I knew Melville's wife well, and was keenly appreciative of her courtesy when she begged me to make their lodgings my 'loafing' place. We met every day for our appointed work. Mrs. Melville generally made the bargains for our carriage, and I would 'settle' with her every night in a regular business-like manner. Those sunny, charming days can never be forgotten, whisking about the narrow streets of Rome in company with the Melvilles.

"In the many pleasant conversations between us, Mrs. Melville would frequently 'run me' on what she chose to call 'my lonely lot' in the world; so that I told her that my fate was in her keeping, and that she must become responsible for it. She clapped her white hands with delight, and assured me that she would ever serve my best interests. One afternoon I returned late from a tedious and lonely tramp through the Catacombs, to find lying on my table a note from Mrs. Melville, which ran something like this: —

" 'Thursday noon, April 4.

"'MY DEAREST FRIEND: We have just received news that George's niece, Eleanor Donald, is to be with us during Holy Week. She will arrive this evening; and I write to tell you to be sure and come to the Via Condotti, and make one of our tea-party. I wish to tell you something about her. She is a splendid girl, about twenty years old, beautiful, intelligent, but somewhat saddened at present by the death of an intimate friend.

"'I know you will like her, and in this connection I wish to say, that, bearing in mind the sacred promise I made to you in regard to the custody of your fate, I deliberately take this means of bringing both of you together. Come by eight o'clock.

"'Your constant friend,

"'GRISELDA MELVILLE.

"'VIA CONDOTTI, Numero 5.'

"I found ten or twelve pleasant people assembled in the Melville salon; two or three young girls, several artists, and some older parties.

"I had good opportunity for observing Miss Donald from the 'corner of my eye' before I was presented. I perceived that she was neatly dressed, in what I presumed would be called half-mourning. She had a comely and delicate figure, and also an air of repose and simplicity which was quite charming. Very gray, quizzical eyes, with marked lashes and eye-brows, a thin, well-shaped nose, a full, round throat, decked with some dainty female 'fluffery,' a blooming complexion, and largish mouth. Artistically speaking, her chin was the best part of her face, being round and well-modeled, with a dimple just in the middle of it when she smiled. I looked at her ears — always a point of especial interest to me — and found them small, with lobes unattached to the cheek.

"Just then Mrs. Melville took me in convoy, and with a quiet inclination of her pretty head, Eleanor Donald and I were made acquainted.

"'May I sit beside you?' said I.

"'I wish you would. I'm so glad to meet you. I've heard your name so often from the Melvilles.'

"'They are very good, I'm sure.'

"'Oh, yes; and they say you are such a traveler. You must come and pilot us about this wonderful city.'

"'Indeed, I shall be proud to. Are you fond of any particular branch of the arts?'

"'Of course I am. As an English girl I like to sketch, and just now I am crazy to see some of the original crayons of the old masters. Do you draw yourself?' said she.

"'A little; at least I try to think that I do.'

"'Then we can sympathize,' she replied, with winsomeness.

"'An Italian sky is very sympathetic.'

"'Yes; one feels in Italy like a new creature. There are so many objects about one to stimulate taste, and fire the imagination, that one's heart is alive to the most charming emotions, unknown in our befogged island!'

"'Were you pleased with Naples?'

"'More than pleased — enchanted.'

"'I wonder if you visited the little church above

the city on the heights — under the supervision of the monks, you know — and saw from there that magnificent view?'

"'Ah, indeed I did. I never shall forget the whole occasion. In the first place, the church itself is too beautiful for anything; and then that view from the Cloisters! It is beyond words; one must behold it in silence!'

"'You remember Capri in the distance?'

"'Of course; and the blue grotto.'

"'And the azure waters of the bay curving into a crescent, and tumbling in graceful breakers on the yellow shore?'

"'And the red-capped sailors dotted about among their nets and fishing-boats!' added she, with delight.

"'And then old Vesuvius smoking lazily in the distance?'

"'Yes; and then you remember, as you stand there, the roar of the city below you comes swelling up the heights into the cloisters!'

"'You have a keen observation, I should judge.'

"'An individual dead to the beauties which cluster about Naples ought never to have the privilege of going there.'

"'Upon my life! I think you're charming! I haven't met with so much appreciative talent since I left Upper Egypt!'

"'Why Upper Egypt?'

"'Because I met there an enthusiast, — an actor, an archaeologist, and photographer, all in one.'

"Go on and tell me all about it.'

"She inspired me with unwonted enthusiasm, and I went on describing the delight of a life on a dahabeah, and the quaint experiences of a winter on the Nile. As I related my ascent of the pyramids, and my descent into Cheops, my moonlight prowls about Luxor and Karnac, my donkey rides to the tombs of the kings, and the Colossi of Thebes, her great gray eyes opened with intelligent interest, and was another thrilling incentive for me to go on. I described to her the delightful sensations of floating down the Nile back to Cairo ; the peculiar brilliancy of the Egyptian moonlight ; the weird appearance of the great bonfires along the shores at night, and the motley appearance of the turbaned sailors, as in their light they listened to the professional story-teller; of the groaning sakias and the mournful shadoof; of the visits to the different mosques in the city; the wonderful performances of the whirling dervishes and the fanatical fakirs; — in fact, all the experiences of the past season flashed back upon my memory, under the influence of her charming society, and I depicted them before her in the most brilliant colors. Time always flies, and that night it sped away with unwonted rapidity, so that we were both startled by the sudden appearance of Mrs. Melville, who said : —

"'Why! where have you both been? we are all out at supper a half an hour ago, and I've come back to get you; did n't you hear it announced?'

"With some confusion, I confessed that I did n't, while my delightful companion, coming to my rescue, gayly added, 'How could we hear, as we were both 'way up' in the top part of Egypt when the servant came in?'

"I gave her my arm and we went in to supper, and I fed her with all the tempting dainties spread out before us. I noticed, however, that she only played with her fork, and seemed to be thinking over the long journey we had just taken together.

"We had become by this time so well acquainted that whenever we met in company we insensibly gravitated together. The delight that I felt at the sight of so many architectural and artistic relics was greatly heightened by the presence of a sympathizing companion. We wandered together through the galleries, and while the rest of the party would stray away into other portions, we often found ourselves seated before the gem of the collection, utterly oblivious to surrounding objects. Never was I so happy before. Never felt I so keen a joy. Up to this time we had said nothing to each other of any particular personal preference, still there was a certain unmistakable exaltation resulting from our mutual presence. Every day that we met, her large gray eyes spoke the kindliest greeting, and whenever we parted, I found myself the joyful possessor of some little bud or flower plucked by her own fair hands.

"Such emotions, when once aroused, seldom go to rest. They smoulder steadily on, involving each moment more of the vital nature.

"'What is this that I feel?' I would often repeat to myself. 'So strange! so utterly foreign to my heart? It is slowly consuming my very life. If I try to speak, I cannot articulate; if I keep silent, I shall die.'

"So the days rolled swiftly by. The family party went regularly on its round of sight-seeing, while she in my company, and I in hers, trotted about the streets together, shopping and lunching, and dining and chatting; all so naturally, all so entirely without reserve. On one occasion it was proposed to visit the Vatican gallery by torch-light; the effect of the flambeaux on the sculptures being

exceptionally fine. So it was agreed that the family in the Via Condotti, together with some pleasant young men, newly arrived from Milan, should
form an agreeable party for this expedition. There
was delicious moonlight at the time, so that we
would have the opportunity of first observing its
weird effect upon the exterior of St. Peter's and the
Vatican, before witnessing the wonders to be un-
veiled to us under the flaring influence of artificial
illumination within their classic walls. Our family,
— I say 'our' family, because I began to consider
myself one of its members, — our family were already engaged to pass that evening with some artistic friends living near the Capitol, and so it was
arranged to visit the Vatican by eight o'clock, and
then drive across the Tiber afterwards, to our
friends upon the hill.

"A person who has formed one of a procession
which has wandered through the silent galleries of
the Vatican, led on by the flickering candle-light,
will remember the strange and mysterious effect
produced upon the silent statues ranged in long
lines on either side. The pale and serious countenances of Olympian Jove and divine Apollo, of
graceful torso, and youthful nymph, under such
influence, produce a most peculiar effect upon
the beholder. The eyes of that speechless, mar-
ble company seem to follow the receding procession with grave inquiry, as if it had broken in
upon their privacy with unwonted license. The

young girl at my side, in obedience to such impressions, clung to my arm as if for protection. Such an experience was not calculated to inspire our company with much hilarity, the absence of which I noticed as we drove by the Castle of St. Angelo, and across the yellow Tiber, to fulfill our engagement.

"The night was somewhat cloudy at times, but soon again our carriage would be flooded by the moonlight.

"After the enjoyment for an hour or two of charming society, — looking over most interesting artistic productions, conversing with intelligent people, and imbibing with it all a sort of beatific emotion, only to be experienced by the enthusiastic traveler in dear old Rome, — the time for our departure drew near.

"Eleanor Donald was seated near the window, and we watched together the bright moon as she sailed in and out of the hurrying clouds, seeming at times to nod and beckon to us from her fairy car.

"'What a night to visit the Coliseum,' said I.

"'Delicious!' replied my companion, 'if I only could!'

"'You know it is a great feat to have visited the grand old ruin at midnight.'

"'Oh, but why can't I?' cried she. 'It isn't a long way from here. I'd give anything I possess to go there.'

"'Why not ask your uncle and aunt; perhaps

they would all like to go, the night is so wonderfully fine.'

" ' Yes,' said she, ' I 'll propose it.'

" She tripped away from where we sat, to the group which occupied the opposite corner, and there I watched her eager and rosy mouth as it unfolded her desired project.

" ' One may not visit Rome but once, and never have such another moonlight as this. Why not all go?'

" ' Why not, indeed?'

" ' Well, come on!'

" And ' come on ' they all agreed to do. We walked. There were eight of us: the uncle and aunt, the two young men from Milan, and the two Miss Langworthys from America, besides Eleanor Donald and myself.

" Insensibly and gradually we became separated from the rest of our party, and took our way toward the old ruin by a path I knew full well. The others went — I never knew exactly where. They either lost their way or else gave up the expedition altogether, intimidated by the lateness of the hour and fear of Roman fever.

" Eleanor Donald and I kept on. I would n't have stopped in my purpose had I met in my path one of the ancient gladiators himself. We gradually neared the imposing old pile, and paused for an instant to admire its gloomy magnificence in the fitful moonlight. Curiously enough I noticed an

amiable-looking and sociable black dog emerge
from the surrounding shadow and attach himself to
our party as if he belonged to us. He wagged his
great tail in a friendly manner, while his panting
breath was the only sound to be heard, as we
passed through the entrance of the Coliseum.

"Here we were at last in a spot so memorable in
the world's history; and what was better, at the
witching hour of midnight; and what was best,
with the girl of all girls on my arm. My graceful
companion hesitated a moment, but then creeping
up a little closer to me, as if for protection, we advanced into the middle of the arena, and seated
ourselves just under the cross which was erected in
this consecrated spot. We sat together, silently
watching the moon send through the clouds and
then sail out of them again; at one time casting
the whole amphitheatre into shadow, then flooding
it with silver light. The dark arched recesses of the
ancient ruin became peopled with invisible forms
created by excited fancy, while the absolute still-

ness which reigned about us acted like a magic
spell.

"'Think,' said I, hardly above a whisper, 'in
this vacant and lonesome spot were once heard the
prayers of dying martyrs mixed with the jargon of
maddened beasts. On this arena the rough gladia-
tor and the delicate Christian woman have died for
their faith!'

"'Yes!' she replied, in a low, tremulous voice:
'isn't it wonderful what grand achievements faith
in God will cause the weakest of us to perform?'

"After a pause I rejoined in the same half-whis-
per: 'It seems to me, with you at my side, though
all the world was mine enemy, there could be a
faith so strong that one might die for it, even in
these later days!' As I said these words a slight
tremor seemed to seize upon her, and I carefully
wrapped the thick mantilla about her delicate
shoulders, whereupon we became silent once more.

"The old black dog was quite social, and lay at
our feet peacefully sleeping in a domestic sort of
way, while the shadow of the cross erected in the
middle of the circus was mercifully thrown directly
over the spot where we sat together.

"We heard a distant clock strike midnight, and
were somewhat awed by the hoot of an owl perched
high up among the shattered stone galleries. The
mystic spell was still about us, which prevented us
from moving, and I looked upon the dear soul at my
side with an interest I can never forget. The pale

light of the moon shone full into her countenance, and I saw her beautiful open gray eyes glistening with tears, and looking, as it were, far away into the future.

"The dews of evening had made her waving tresses dank and heavy, which transformed her for the moment into one of those beautiful creatures who had perished for her creed two thousand years ago. If I ever were influenced by a high and noble sentiment it was at that moment.

"I said, 'I have loved you with all the strength of my nature from the first moment I met you in the Via Condotti.'

"'I know it.' whispered this loved one.

"'How did you know it, dear child?'

"'I don't know. I—' She was silently weeping.

"'Can you put any faith in me, dear Eleanor?'

"'Faith! Indeed I can; that is, I suppose so. I hardly know what to say. I am—I—think— would n't we better go home now?' said Eleanor, in a sweet, tremulous tone, while a little tear fell at our feet on that same soil which had been drenched so many times with the tears and blood of persecuted Christians.

"Yes! Certainly we will; but you are not affronted with me, are you, for saying I loved you, Eleanor?'

"'Affronted! How could I? It makes me happy —so happy; but you see I'm not exactly myself.

You won't say any more now, will you? Wait a few days; let me think about it, whether or not, you know, that's a good fellow!'

"'No, dear child. I'll do nothing to trouble you. Let me put your shawl on better. It's all askew. —there. Isn't that more comfortable?'

"'Yes!' thanks. Come, let's go!'

"'Wait one moment.' cried I. 'You've dropped your handkerchief. It wouldn't do to leave that, would it?"

"No, indeed. I need *that*. It's so cold, you know.' She said this with a sweet, teary smile, scarcely knowing what she did. She looked so like a young goddess, with her beatified countenance, her bright eye and her trembling lips, that I could scarcely restrain myself from frantically clasping her to my bosom.

"We arose, however, from our places beside the great cross. She grasped my arm with both her little cold white hands, and we paced across the ancient amphitheatre in perfect silence, followed by our trusty friend the black dog, and so passed out beyond its portals on our way toward the city.

"As we strode along, nought was heard but the heavy footfalls of the man, mixed with the light and quicker steps of his companion. Each mind was too busy to articulate its cogitations, yet Eleanor clung, sometimes almost convulsively, to my arm, while my own knees trembled violently all the way.

"How I reached my lodgings, after leaving my companion at hers, I know not. The whole experience was like some delightful reverie, which took until the next morning's sun came shining directly in my face to convince me that I was actually in the flesh and not far away in the spirit.

"After such a transaction, could it be said that there was 'nothing between us?' Two hearts' secrets had been laid bare before 'God and this company' of invisible spirits in that ancient theatre, which could never be retracted. And so it happened that a few more plain words, a little ring from off my watch-chain on her tiny finger, and the deed seemed to be accomplished. Eleanor Donald told me that she loved me, and we became, if not actually, at least prospectively, pledged to each other for life.

"Existence in Rome, during the solemn ceremonies of Holy Week, under such circumstances, became clothed with stranger and more serious importance.

"Mr. and Mrs. Melville suspected what they officially did not know, and, good souls, left us to enjoy the bright, fleeting moments together. So it was decreed that Eleanor Donald and I could go about the Holy City like two young birds.

"There is no affection so sure and solid as to be beyond the reach of peradventure. It is that very quality of apprehension which makes a youthful passion full of surprises.

"Reciprocal attachment of years' standing may

be an old joke, but that which characterizes newly
discovered reciprocity is quite a different affair.
Then it is that a tear is a mute declaration of a
life's secret; a sigh contains a continent of bliss;
a pressure, the destiny of two lives.

"There was a delicate reticence in the nature of
Eleanor Donald which repressed any marked ex-

pression of happiness, but she exhibited her fond-
ness for me in a way that increased both my faith-
fulness and respect. Parents were to be consulted.
Time was to bear its weight upon our contract.
Calm judgment was to sit on its merits; in fact
there were hosts of horrible peradventures which
commenced to raise their ugly forms before us the
very moment when the field was won. 'Heaven

will decide.' 'Have faith in me!' were the cheery words of Eleanor Donald, as we parted from each other on the eve before Palm Sunday.

"I shall never forget Easter-week in Rome. No! not if all the other events of my life be blotted out, this week will stand in my memory as a most sacred epoch. We talked but little of our mutual secret, but went about together, to and from St. Peter's, delighted observers of its great feasts.

"We saw the Pope distribute the palms on Palm Sunday. We were part of the great crowd within the church when his Holiness was borne into the cathedral in his chair of state, on the shoulders of his cardinals. We heard the flourish of the silver trumpets. We witnessed the washing of the pilgrims' feet, and saw the High Pontiff present each one with a bouquet of flowers and a purse of money. Arm in arm we pressed through that tremendous crowd of well-dressed strangers, up the stairway and into the chamber where the Pope waited, as a servant, upon these same pilgrims, in imitation of the Saviour at the Last Supper. Together we stood in the piazza San Pietro, among the mighty throng collected there, and bowed our heads when the Pope blessed the populace from the balcony ; and finally, we listened with bated breath to the solemn 'Miserere" within the dimly lighted hall of the Sistine Chapel.

"How beautiful she appeared among the bevy of richly-dressed women which filled the dais within

the cathedral on those holy festivals! The black
veil was especially becoming to her, while her slender figure was easily distinguished from among the
countesses and ambassadors' wives, by its graceful
lines. Before breakfast each morning the church
would be filled with these beauties from every land,
while, according to regulation, men in full evening
attire wandered about the immense edifice with
opera-hat and white cravat. A curious medley:
but so unique, so idiosyncratic!

"The Melville party was to leave Rome on the
Tuesday after Easter, for Germany, so that the
evening of Easter Monday would be the last time I
should see them until we met in Paris in the approaching autumn.

"It was arranged between Eleanor and me that,
as a matter of mutual trial, there should be but
little correspondence, and that all things should be
left as they were until we met again. I acquiesced
at once in this wise request, as it commended itself
both to my judgment and my desire to please her.

"On Easter Monday evening the grand exhibition of the illumination of St. Peter's was witnessed
by all of us, first from the piazza in front of the
cathedral, and then again from the summit of the
Pincian Hill, where in the starlight the mighty
edifice, flashing from pediment to cross, looked like
some huge ark floating upon a waste of waters.

"Ten o'clock came. The show was over. The
moment arrived for our party to break up. After

bidding both the Melvilles a warm 'good-by,' with a solemn promise to meet at the 'Trois Frères' on the fifth of the next September. I alighted from the carriage and went round to the side where Eleanor Donald was seated. I took her soft hand in both of mine, and whispered, 'Good-by, dearest Eleanor; we meet in Paris in September." By the dim starlight I saw her pale countenance look earnestly upon me for an instant, and then bending down her little face for me to kiss, she murmured, 'Have faith in me. Heaven will take care of both of us. God bless you until we meet again!'

"I entered the Via Ripetta on foot, while the Melville carriage rolled quickly away and turned the corner.

"I loitered about Rome for a week or more after the rush of departing strangers was over, and at last took up my own line of march for the north. From Rome I went by diligence to Bologna, and then to Venice. The moon had gone away, but I didn't miss it half so much as I did the 'casta diva' whom I had lost. So, wrapped in my French caban, I was rowed along the gloomy lagunes, under the Rialto, until I became plunged in melancholy. From Venice I took flight to Milan, and by the last of May started over the St. Gothard Pass to Lucerne, and so on until I reached gay Paris. Here, the soldiers, the high-capped *bonnes*, the little *grisettes*, and the orange-trees were as thick as butterflies in the Tuileries' gardens.

"The Langworthys were in Paris, and from them I heard of the Melvilles. They were passing a month in Germany in company with some friends from England. I left Paris the next week, and after 'knocking about' the Pyrenees for a month, I went to the Tyrol and spent another: then a week or so at St. Moritz in the Engadine. I came over the perpendicular Gemmi, down to Thun: then 'kited' quickly along so as to reach Paris again by September.

"I occupied once more my old rooms in the Rue Neuve St. Augustin, and found that Monsieur Berger, the concierge, wore the same queer worsted cap, and kept the same dirty monkey as of yore, while his court-yard was as dismal as ever.

"Dining one day at the Café Voisin, I saw in the 'Galignani' the arrival of the Melvilles at the Hôtel Bristol. There they were, sure enough. 'Mr. and Mrs. George Melville and maid.' Miss Donald and maid.'

"I looked at this announcement long and anxiously. Here we were again almost face to face, but with this lapse of six months between us! Had this interval altered our relations together? I must confess that simple announcement was 'too much' for me, and it was a moment before I could command myself sufficiently to sip my claret without spilling it.

"'Of course I must go there,' said I to myself, 'this very night, and within an hour!'"

"How human vanity always steps in on such occasions. How scrupulously it bids one deck himself, and tie his cravat, and see that his appearance is entirely *comme il faut!*

"I was ushered into the salon of the Melvilles at the Hôtel Bristol, and greeted by them both

with the warmest effusion. Miss Donald arose from her seat, where she was sitting with a young gentleman whom I had never seen before. She shook my hand very pleasantly; asked me how I had passed the summer; said she had been walking over the Bernese Oberland, and then introduced

me to her companion, to whom I made respectful
obeisance. After this we sat again, and the Melvilles and I ran rapidly over the events which had
transpired since we all were in Rome together.

"Melville told me that they were now a party of
five: himself and wife and Miss Donald with Mr.
and Miss Murgatroyd, intimate friends from England, who were to be with them until their return
home.

"Miss Donald continued talking so earnestly with
Mr. Murgatroyd, and for such a length of time,
that my heart commenced beating with vague fore-
bodings, and my temples to throb with suspicious
anxiety. She came forward, however, soon after,
and asked me how I was, and said they were very
glad to see me again. My voice must have trembled
at her apparent composure and forgetfulness of our
delicate relations to each other, — which was probably betrayed in my reply to her inquiry, — for she
remarked in a low tone, —

"'I have suffered much since we met. This
gentleman is a very old friend of ours, and you
must know I have settled a little difference which
existed between us for a long time, and that has
made me very happy.'

"I told her that I rejoiced that she had done so,
for I didn't see how one could live at variance with
anybody and be happy.

"'No!' said she, 'especially if he is a very *dear*
friend!'"

" 'Do you remain long in Paris?' she added.

" 'Long?' said I. 'Long!' perfectly astounded at her nonchalance. 'I really can't say; it depends — upon' —

"My voice utterly failed me. I could not speak. I looked at her in astonishment — almost tearfully for a moment — and she met my eye with a quiet, unsuspicious gaze, and then remarked, —

" 'You must be sure to go to the Ambassador's to-morrow night. We shall all be there, and the music will be delicious.'

" 'I shall surely be there,' said I. 'But have you forgotten our visit at Rome?'

" 'How lovely! It seems a hundred years ago!'

" 'And the Coliseum; has *it* faded from memory?'

" 'Oh, horrible! I wouldn't go there again for worlds! I wonder I didn't catch the Roman fever!'

" 'Have your feelings changed toward me, Eleanor?'

" 'Since when?'

" 'Since then!'

" 'I was an awful scare-cat that night. I acted like a child!'

" 'I see plainly,' said I, 'that you are determined to ignore the past.'

" 'You know what Longfellow says: "Let the dead past bury its dead." But be sure to come to the Ambassador's to-morrow. Good-night!'

"I went back to my lodgings, perfectly unmanned. I sat by the open window, just as I was, in my evening dress, for hours — thinking — thinking. I was pallid with sadness; and like a child, so thoroughly crushed, so terribly cut up.

"Said I, aloud, 'I did n't know there *were such* women in the world: so angelic to look upon, so damnable to have anything to do with.'

"The cold, gray morning found me still in ball costume: but with the new day a stern and different spirit possessed me. 'Love swells like the Solway, but ebbs like its tide!' I quietly arose and went to my chamber; carefully bathed and dressed myself, and went through the daily routine without a word — without a murmur.

"In the evening I arrayed myself scrupulously, and made it a point to go to the Ambassador's. Eleanor Donald was there, looking radiant in roses and tulle. It made no impression upon me. When the music 'struck up' for dancing, I approached her — almost rudely — and looking straight in her eye, said: 'You must dance with me once more, and for the last time in this world!'

"She gazed at me almost wildly. The color faded from her cheeks, while, with an almost agonized expression, she faltered, — 'Certainly, if you wish it.'

"'We stand here,' said I. I led her through the 'Lancers' with a supercilious smile on my lip, but speechless. I escorted her back, frightened, to her seat with almost exaggerated courtesy.

"She commenced to say: 'But are n't we going to' — But I cut her short by, 'We are going to part forever! That's what we are going to do,' and left her.

"I have had the ill-luck to meet her twice since that baleful night; but I recognized her no more than I would a stock or a stone. She was unworthy the name of woman; for, curse her, did n't she nearly break my heart?"

Cynicus Donce stopped reading the MSS.

"Good heavens!" cried the Nervous Exhaustionist from out the new hammock, "is it finished?"

"That's the whole of it," replied Mr. Douce.

The company was lost in thought. The lady with a history wiped her eyes. Mrs. George Madison Taggart looked vacantly over the hills: she was thinking of her treatment of the poor man who was engaged to her when she threw him over for the wealthy Taggart. The others kept silent.

"Whoever this creature was," said the sympathizing Amelia, "he had a pretty hard time of it."

"Eleanor Donald couldn't have been a true woman," sighed Consuelo, the Countess; "no *true* woman would ever have treated a man like that."

"What is a *true* woman?" asked Cynicus, blandly.

"Why, a true woman is one who never"—

"Flirts?" suggested Cynicus.

"Not exactly flirts, but one who never tells a man she loves him, and then"—

"What! Never?" interpolated Mr. Douce.

"No! never tells a man she loves him and then deliberately marries another: she never does. Does she, girls?"

"No, of course she never does. Whoever heard of such a thing?" cried all the unmarried girls.

"All ladies on this lawn," said Mr. Lawrence, "who have once acknowledged their love for one man, and then have not afterwards left him in the lurch for another lover, will please hold up their hands."

They were all just about to raise them, when Benjamin's great tea-bell providentially rang on the long piazza, and the fascinating bevy of true women marched in to supper. The sweet little Hildegarde was quite interested in the story, and staying behind, asked Cynicus if that was *really* the whole of the MSS. Mr. Douce said there was one chapter more, which seemed to be an experience in Switzerland; and he promised to read it to the ladies some " off " afternoon.

CHAPTER II.

IT was not always Sunday in Paradise. There were six days during which the varied secular amusements had full swing; but when the first day of each week *did* arrive, the inhabitants of Paradise welcomed it with becoming respect. They donned their starchiest habiliments. They adjusted their countenances to the correct angle, and they marched down the south road as decorously as good Christians ought to do.

There is something very characteristic in the way Sunday is observed in New England. The Puritanical flavor of the last century, that pious

grimness which made religion a business as well as
a duty, has worn itself sufficiently away to leave
at the present day only a suspicion of its former
presence. This suspicion, however, still permeates
the social fabric, and lends to it an impressive element of distinctness not to be found elsewhere.
Little boys and big ones feel as if on that day
their best clothes and their best manners were to
be aired, so whenever the sturdy yeomanry of
New England "dress up" they look unusually solemn and unusually uncomfortable. Now this is
all well enough if the change of demeanor and
change of dress would not stop here, but would just
go on, altering bad habits and making over bad
hearts into good ones. But observation leads us to
remark that Sunday, of all the days in the week, is
the one when if anybody *is* cross, that body is *cross-
est* then; and if there *are* misunderstandings, it is
on Sunday morning just before one goes to church.
In Paradise, however, that lovely spot, these frag-
mentary disputes were almost unknown, and the
morning of the first day was generally the most
peaceful portion of the week. The city clothes
and the white laces, the nodding plumes and the
silver-clasped prayer-books of the guests, blended
lovingly together with the more modest attire of
the villagers; and both bodies of Christians trotted
amicably along the brown roads together, making
a beautiful picture. All of our Paradisiacal friends
were very good people: they thought highly of

their church, and held well-defined views on all religious matters : but some of them were unable to
attend church. The Beautiful N. E., for instance,
was prevented by her nervous exhaustion from going there regularly. Besides the necessity of quieting her nerves, there were many other little things
to be done before she was ready to start : so that
church time was come and often gone before she
had put on her gloves, or even her right boot.
Then the hour was much too early for invalids such
as she. The seats were far too hard : and, worst
of all, she was regularly seized every Sunday morning with an undefined horror of entering a crowded
building. She feared that so soon as she should
reach her crimson-cushioned pew, away down the
broad aisle, she would certainly faint, and have to
be carried out over the heads of the whole congregation, by all the men, particularly by that tall
fright of a creature who sat just across from her
pew, in number 112, and looked at her so imper-
tinently whenever she *did* go to the sanctuary.
Therefore, the mere mention of church made the
Beautiful N. E. sea-sick. All these misfortunes,
however, did not alter " her views " on church matters, which were very pronounced. But our good
friend, Mr. Cynicus Douce, was in his place every
Sunday as regularly as a clock. In the city, he sat
in the same seat where his father and his grandfa-
ther (the gentleman who fought in the great Revo-
lution) had sat before him, so that he did not thank

anybody who presumed to offer him advice on ordinary religious questions.   Mr. Douce was sensible withal.   He knew that ministers were mortals,
even if they *were* pious, and that they required
quite as much to eat and drink as other Christians
did, if not more.   He quarreled with those people
who, having fifteen or twenty thousand a year to
spend on themselves, speak of poor parsons with a
lean wife and eight hungry children living on a
thousand a year and house-rent to pay besides, as
being in " comfortable circumstances," and needing
no " outside help."

He sympathized with them, even when he ob-
jected to some of their narrow views and their oc-
casional unfitness for their vocation.   Mr. Douce
had a singular creed, which consisted, among other
things, in this: that nobody should be allowed to
preach the gospel to sinners but those who knew,
from their own bitter experience, what sin actually
was: who had been buffeted and tossed about by
the temptations of modern civilization; who had
been caught in the golden snare of worldliness, and
who by all this experience had become convinced
that the inevitable end of it all was misery and
ashes.   He did not believe in allowing inexperienced and harmless young men, who had been tied
to their mothers' apron-strings until they went to
the seminary, who had never known what a terrible thing to withstand temptation was, and what
herculean effort was required to beat back the

devil when he appeared as an "angel of light:" he did not approve of such young gentlemen, though decked in all the smartness of sacerdotal habiliment, delivering a mellifluous discourse from some unintelligible text of St. Paul's, to hoary-headed but well-dressed sinners ranged in the pews before them.   And this simply because he believed it did no good, but possibly some harm.

He reserved these unpractical ideas to impart to his dear friend Lady Angela, who listened to him in an amused sort of way, as if she half believed what he said.

This sweet woman was always apologizing for everybody's short-comings, and was shocked when anything was spoken derogatory to the church or its belongings.   Trained in the old-fashioned methods which accepted as facts everything descended from the Fathers, she was slow to examine too critically these unchallenged truths.   But Lady Angela was a very sensible woman: indeed her good sense overcame her emotions, so that it was difficult to deceive her by anything inherently a sham.   And although truthful to a fault, if such a thing be possible, yet (like the rest of her sex) she longed to have some unimpeachable authority in religious matters to lean upon; but when anything was actually absurd, nobody saw it quicker, and nobody condemned it sooner than Lady Angela.   Mr. Cynicus Douce, therefore, had a listener who, while she did not easily accept all of his (as she termed them)

"wild theories," yet was keen and clear-headed
enough to perceive at once when he chanced upon
a kernel of truth. Their discussions were often of
a very lively character, and the welfare of the little
parish of Paradise came in for a goodly share of
attention.

There was one lady in the small community who
took even more interest than either Lady Angela
or Mr. Donce did in its spiritual welfare. She was
possessed of good mental capacity, but, if the truth
were told, was somewhat narrow in "her views" on
church matters. This lady was no other than Miss
Ennice Smart, a Church-woman from her birth.
She was like all good people who think on one subject incessantly. It becomes at last the great object of their life. This object to Miss Smart was
"The Church." She held the no uncommon belief
that the whole truth about sacred matters was discovered, like a nugget of gold, in the Middle Ages.
She believed that every specimen of the Christian
Father was an exemplary Christian; that he never
wrangled with his brothers, was never selfish nor
bigoted, but lived a pure and virtuous life. She
held also that, gathered together in fraternal council, these amiable and unmilitant men had discovered what was best (in the way of dogma and
creed) for the guidance of the Church for all ages
to come. Moreover, Miss Smart, applying these
views to the modern Church establishment, nar-
rowed her ideas down to one creed, one branch,

one sect of that branch, one seminary of that sect,
and finally to one priest of that seminary. On all
other subjects she was very funny, very clever, and
very good company, and her conversation, therefore, was always crisp and original.

As might be inferred, with all these different elements in the community, it became a somewhat difficult task to decide upon an acceptable incumbent
for the little parish of Paradise.

The Beautiful N. E., the Lady Angela, Mr. Douce,
and Miss Smart were only types of the many forms
of opinion which would certainly be called upon
to decide this delicate question.

The summer had proved a very hot and dusty
one in Paradise, and the usually damp and brown
roads were now merely heaps of white dust which
every passing carriage sent whirling into the air.
Like the dust, so this question was sure to be raised
whenever a passing remark from any casual observer suggested the discussion.

Such was the condition of things when it was
understood that a Sunday morning service would be
held in the new edifice, which had at last reached
completion, and that a possible incumbent of the
little parish was to preach to them on that occasion.

This dainty memorial chapel in Paradise, with
its rough rubble walls, its high-pitched roof, its
tinted windows, and its brick trimmings, was most
picturesque.

As one approached it from the south road, or even coming in the opposite direction, its appearance, nestled among the tall pines, was very prepossessing. It produced just that quieting, grave, and loving impression which one desires to feel creeping over him as he enters the portals of a country

church. The robins and the orioles were twittering among the dense foliage which surrounded the sacred edifice, while a peaceful Sunday stillness spread itself over the green, undulating fields in its vicinity. The pews in the little chapel were pleasant to sit in. They had just the right bevel for both ease and reverence, which is a good recom-

mendation for any church. The several articles of
a memorial character, which kind hands and loving hearts had added, were exceedingly appropriate,
while the chancel appointments bore the mark of
an educated, ecclesiological taste. Nothing was
wanting but the minister. Who shall he be? With
what stripe of churchmanship shall he be identi-
fied? The high, the low, the broad, the ritualistic,
the high and dry Connecticut, or the low and liberal
evangelical?—vital questions to the Paradise we
are speaking of, however unimportant they may be
to that other and better one. As was very natural,
there was some excitement among the members of
the little parish on this subject.

The Rev. Mr. Cowl was first invited to preach,
but he was found much too "high" for Paradise.
Some of the parishioners were horrified, and said
"he did everything," whatever that expression might
mean. Then the Rev. George Fenner ascended the
pulpit, but he was just as much too "low" as Mr.
Cowl was too "high." He did not lay stress enough
on the authority of the Church to please Paradise.
Then came Father Emerson, who was one of the
order of the missionary brothers. His great hobby
was preaching the gospel in foreign parts. "Paro-
chial missions, and diocesan missions, and domestic
missions, were all well enough," said Father Emerson, "but in order to evangelize the world we must
begin with Christianizing the Chinese, and then
"work this way." Home fields would fall into

line the instant that foreign lands had been plowed
over." Paradise, being a "home field," had no use
for the Rev. Father Emerson. After him, a little
Mr. Holly, from East Ipswich, came to the village.
He was invited to preach, but could not be prevailed upon to wear the surplice at sermon time,
insisting on putting on the old black scholastic
gown, long discarded, and much too voluminous for
his short stature. This so displeased Miss Eunice
Smart that she walked straight out of the new
church in face of the whole congregation.

An experience like this was trying, since it was
very necessary for the welfare of Paradise that
a clergyman should be selected, not only acceptable to the members of the parish itself, but also
to the large crowd of strangers who frequented
the village during the summer months.

At last a lady from New York city suggested
the name of the Rev. Ambrose St. Julien as a most
suitable person, she thought, for the position. "St.
Julien," she said, "was just graduated from the
seminary. He was young and unmarried, two good
recommendations, which always interest the old,
and, she might add, the young as well. Besides,
the reverend gentleman's churchmanship lay mid-
way between the two extremes: not so high as
to be displeasing to Captain Americus Topdressing,
the richest farmer in Paradise, nor so low as to
interfere seriously with the religious convictions
of Miss Eunice Smart. She advised the committee

to invite him to fill the pulpit the next Sunday,
which would be the eighth after Trinity.   So the
Rev. Ambrose St. Julien,
having just entered the di-
aconate, was summoned to
Paradise as the guest of the
New York lady on the hill-
top.

The Lady Angela, who had
for many years interested
herself in the welfare of the
little parish, played the new
organ, while Miss Lucy sang
soprano, and Cousin Edith
took the alto part of the
church music, every Sunday.
These obliging volunteers
were always rummaging the
different hymnals for the
most appropriate hymns for
each service, and had selected the 190th and the
202d as the proper ones for this particular occasion.

The morning was auspicious.   White cumulus
clouds floated lazily over the zenith propelled by
gentle zephyrs.   The buzz of the crickets was
heard in the fields.   The yellow butterflies fluttered
uncertainly before one's pathway, while a shim-
mering haze in the valleys proclaimed a warm day.
The south road was alive with scores of gayly

dressed people in flaring hats, and fresh-looking
costumes. There were children with starched
frocks and dainty prayer-books; mild-eyed lassies
with immaculate gloves and fluffy jabots; and
jaunty cavaliers, with all the smart extravagances
of neckerchief and stocking which characterize the
toilet of the modern Adonis. One of the prettiest
sights in the world is such a youthful company, zig-
zagging in delightful disorder down a country road
of a Sunday morning. A large delegation from
the "hill"—a precious load—trotted by in Benjamin's big wagon, while Claude and Cynthia, Cupid and Psyche, Apollo and Diana, with heads down
and parasols up, lagged in stately parallels across
the road in the rear.

The gay-colored crowd vanished, one after
another, over the threshold of the new stone
chapel, suggesting to the mind the sparks which,
as children, we used to watch "go out" one after
another on the nursery hearth. It always takes a
certain number of twistings and turnings before
any congregation is fairly settled. If one man
happens to cough over on the east side of the
church, two or three others must need take advantage of this fracture of silence to "ka-hem" and
sneeze over on the west. There are always two
or three late comers, too, who make a great flurry
getting into the front pews. The two strange boys,
who have "no business" there, must first be routed
out, and then the stout lady tries to file past the

thin lady, who is undecided whether to go out or
in, and thereupon follows the usual teetering, which
the congregation watches in mournful silence.

Every lady is fanning herself; every man is wip-
ing his brow; every boy is looking over the back
of the pew.   Dear, near-sighted Lady Angela, with

her eyes 'way down to the keys, is performing one
of her most approved "voluntaries" on the new
organ. The last note is hushed. The Rev. Ambrose St. Julien enters from the robing-room and
kneels at the new chancel-rail.

He is a tidy-looking young gentleman, in white
cravat, and new black sacerdotalish garments,
appropriate enough to his position as one of the
"inferior clergy." Twenty-two is about his age.
Devout and hungry eyes look upon the congregation, while a large, ascetic, and celibate mouth
shows great capacity for suffering. To an impar-
tial observer — not the New York lady — he appears to be an inexperienced, callow, but devout

young man, bent upon what he calls his "mission
in life," an enthusiastic individual who has "convictions" collated from the writings of some eminent
mediaeval authority whom he has taken as his pat-
tern. From this fountain he has derived his creed,
which teaches him, among other things, that the
instant he "took orders" he mounted a pedestal
separate and apart from all lower sinners; that
from this elevation he became suddenly invested
with a knowledge of matters of which, to be sure,
he knows nothing by experience, but which he believes has miraculously descended upon him through
the two hands of his diocesan. He read the service in a voice which, if he had used after church,
he would have been hurried off to an insane retreat.
He jumbled the words all up together as if they
were Latin or some other foreign tongue, and if he
laid emphasis upon anything, it was the conjunc-
tions and the articles.

He mounted the pulpit at last, and gave out his
text in a scholastic undertone: —

"And seeing the multitude he went up into a mountain." —
MATT. v. 1.

"I wish to speak to you, my friends, for a brief
space this morning, on the exclusiveness of the
founder of the Christian faith. The religion expounded by the Son of Mary is not exactly what
the popular idea, prevalent nowadays, makes it
out to be. It is a priceless treasure, not a common
boon. It is beyond the price of rubies, and can-

not be purchased with money. We must infer,
therefore, that only a privileged few of the earth's
inhabitants will be able to enjoy its inestimable
benefits, and become the happy owners of this immortal inheritance. Nowhere throughout the New
Testament is it shown that the author of Christianity was a person who ever mixed with the common people as a companion.

"As a rabbi or teacher, he was accounted one of
an exclusive sect among the Jews. It is true that
he walked about the streets of Jerusalem and Judea, but he walked unattended, except by a chosen
few of his disciples. The rabble were afraid of
him. They looked askance at him, as one separate
and apart from their own rank in life.

"We must remember that he was no ordinary
citizen, but the 'Prince of Peace;' and his murder-
ers called him 'the King of the Jews.' So when
interpreting the New Testament we need to keep
constantly in our minds that this wonderful teacher
was set apart, even by his countrymen, as above
and beyond all his fellows. Hedged about by that
divine right of kingship, he naturally kept himself
exclusive. As a consequence of all this exclusiveness his religion is an exclusive religion. When we
read that, among his other attributes, he came into
the world as the sinner's friend, it will not do to
make the interpretation too large. These texts
should properly read, 'He was friend of such sinners as should be saved,' and 'he came into the

world to befriend repentant sinners of the Church."
This version would bring it down to about the limit
allowed by the most conservative church-writers of
the present day. All people cannot expect to par-
take of such inestimable benefits, but only such
good churchmen as are predestinated, elected, and
preordained by the eternal fiat of Omnipotence.
In support of this view let me quote some unmistakable texts bearing on this point : —

"In the twentieth chapter of Matthew and part of
the sixteenth verse, we read, 'For many be called,
but few chosen:' that is, the 'elected' few are the
only ones to enter. The rest must bear the result
of their own misfortune.

"Again, in Acts i. verse 47, 'And the Lord
added to the church daily such as should be saved.'
The word 'such' in the Greek, freely translated,
clearly means to *limit* the number to a chosen few,
an exclusive few.

"Again, we have another instance of this exclusiveness in the incident of the raising of the
daughter of Jairus, where it is said that, '*When*
the people were put forth *he* went in,' etc.

"And finally, — for I could go on multiplying
the instances which go to prove my proposition, —
finally, I adduce this extract from Matthew xiii. 2,
'And great multitudes were gathered together unto
him, so that he went into a ship and sat.' This
forcibly indicates his desire to get away from the
multitude. He went into a ship and *sat* apart,

while the multitude probably *stood*, as before their superior, on the shore. And then lastly, the text we have chosen, ' And seeing the multitude he went up into a mountain.' Now it may be asked — and it is a pretty important question — who are these elected few, this exclusive company of prophets and martyrs? Clearly not many of the οἱ πολλοί, even though this πολλοί were a repentant πολλοί, unless peradventure they happened to be of those elected few, — those worthy ones who are found doing his will in his holy Church. His holy Church! That Church which he ordained, and which has come down to us unbroken, through much tribulation and blood; through evil report and good report, from the Petrine foundation of the Christian era.

" It will not do to hug to one's self the idea that because an individual has attached himself to some of those irresponsible bodies — those so-called Christians, those numerous sects in the world, governed by conferences, councils, or other secular modes — that thereby he is within the pale of the Christian Church, as we understand this Christian Church to be, — because this hallucination will lead him into fatal error. Those and those only are members of his Church who belong to *his elect*. They are those who conform to the rites and ceremonies, the historic dogmas, and the most accepted creeds, which have come down to us in regular gradation from the blessed Peter himself; or have been promulgated by the Church from time to time, through

her authorized channels. They are those who
take, unquestioned, what the Church holds to be
pure doctrine, — if they can discover what that is,
— and who accept its assertions without cavil, and
obey its commands without reserve. I pity all
those cavilers, agnostics, and free-thinkers who dare
to judge for themselves of such matters, and who
are bold enough to say that many of our inestimable rites and usages, which have descended to us
from the blessed mediaeval era, are false inferences
of sinful men from what the great Teacher himself
inculcated. I weep for those erring sons who per-
sist in saying that the Great Christian Exemplar
never expounded a creed, established a dogma, nor
drew up a liturgy during his ministry, and that
he only went about healing the sick, casting out
devils, and begging everybody to love his neighbor as himself; leaving the wrangling about dogma
to weak-minded and vacillating churchmen; and,
moreover, I defy these degenerate sons of the
Church who flippantly say that all our precious
and increasingly gorgeous ritual, our elaborate and
symbolic ceremonies, are not at all in accordance
with the simple teachings of the Great Master
himself, but only the outcroppings of pharisaical
diets and vainglorious councils. As good churchmen let us dismiss from our minds all such mischievous assertions as unworthy of serious consid-
eration. If the sacred truth concerning these matters was not discoverable by those blessed saints

and broad-minded martyrs who lived at an age
when men gave up their whole lives to their sacred
work of reading and flagellating, surely in this gen-
eration, which is so much farther removed from the
date of the Christian era, and at a time when men's
minds are warped by what is popularly called 'the
right of private judgment.' — it is twice the harder
task to reach the meaning of those eternal verities.
It is worthy to note, that *faith* in our holy Church
must come in to sustain us just here. This faith
must be greater than a mustard-seed to avail anything. Surely the authority of a church, episcopal
in its government, and which can be traced at least
as far back as the second century, if not farther, —
and what do a hundred years, more or less, matter in so vast an inquiry, — surely such authority
should have a weight in our minds so strong as to
silence forever all such assaults of agnostic infi-
delity as have been referred to.

"By this authority then, we say, that an episcopal
form of church government is the only true vehicle
of Christian doctrine; that it and it alone is authorized to speak from time to time to the world; that
this government is a conservative and an exclusive
government, and that this authority is above 'prin-
cipalities, and powers, and things present, and things
to come.' We have then but to hear her teachings
as explained and expounded by her anointed priests
to obey them. When we contemplate the hundreds
of millions of the earth's inhabitants, comparatively

a small number will be brought under the saving
influence of the Church; in other words, be found
numbered among the elect; but then this very fact
agrees perfectly with the idea which we enunci-
ated at the commencement of this discourse, — the
blessed exclusiveness of our particular faith. We
read neither in the Old nor the New Testament
that these chosen few, these elect, will be other than
that preordained and surpliced company which cluster about the eternal aegis of episcopal authority
inside the chancel-rail. Safe within this exclusive
barrier, they will be kept aloof from the surging
tide of conglomerate sinners, who vainly cling to
their straws of safety on the outside, and will met-
aphorically, and in their own poor way, try to copy
their great prototype, who, 'seeing a multitude,
went up into a mountain.'

"There is thus much to cheer those who rejoice
in the conservatism of our hereditary Church. We
know that *we* in the Church are safe, whatever
may happen to those deluded souls on the outside.
We can only say to such, that we have pointed out
to them their folly; we have directed them to the
most unquestioned and approved channels of salvation; we have marked the proper collects and
prayers made and provided for just such cases.
We can do no more. Nothing remains but the de-
nunciation of the prophet: 'Ephraim is joined to
idols; let him alone!' But let us, the chosen
few, continue on in our blessed work. Be sober;

be diligent; be exclusive. Tell people outside the Church they are lost. Teach our children the rubrics and the symbolic significance of the Christian year. Leave the door of the Church just open enough to facilitate the idea of Christian union. The Church will do everything for this consummation of its hopes which is consistent with its ancient conservatism: but if Jews, Turks, nonconformists, and infidels willfully refuse to enter, it is their own fault and not ours: we cannot go out to meet them. They have the Prayer-book and the hymnal. 'Let them hear them!' 'And seeing a multitude, he went up into a mountain.' Amen!"

The congregation slowly separated.

"Well," said Lawrence to Lady Angela, "what do you think of the Rev. Ambrose St. Julien?"

Lady A. "I think he preaches what he thinks he believes."

Lawrence. "I think what he preaches is the most consummate bosh I ever heard. Look at the absurdity of the application of his text: then the perfect *non-sequitur* of the whole of it. He must be an idiot."

"No," answered Lady Angela, "a man with one idea tortures everything, even texts from Scripture, into a meaning which shall conform to his hobby."

"Why," said Lawrence, laughing immoderately, "hear him coolly telling us that the Saviour, seeing the multitude about him, went up into a mountain in order to get away from the vulgar herd! He might as well have said that when Moses was ordered to 'speak unto the children of Israel that they go forward,' that before that time the whole nation was actually walking backwards."

Mr. Douce remarked, " There is one good thing about him : he said, in so many words, what I have heard lots of parsons infer, but did n't dare speak out."

" Yes," replied Lawrence, " this word 'inference' has caused a deal of mischief in the world ; especially in religious matters. People are all the time inferring that what the Scripture says in so many words it does n't mean : that the real signification, in the original Greek, is exactly opposite from what it is translated in our version ; and, therefore, what it seems to say, it does n't say at all."

" I want to cry," said Cynicus.

" Why ? " said Lady Angela.

Cyn. " Because this little parson is so narrow. I pity him from the bottom of my heart ; for he is looking through the large end of the telescope, and don't know it. What an idea he has of the Christian religion, to be sure."

Lawrence. " You 're right, Douce. Such a creature would roast his own grandmother alive, if she did n't subscribe to some particular rubric on some particular page of the revised canons. What we want *in* the Church is a little more ordinary common sense."

Cyn. "What we want *out* of the Church is just this narrow sort of doctrine."

"I want to cry once more," continued Cynicus.

Lawrence. "What! Again?"

Cyn. "Yes; because as we don't believe in a Pope, we can't prevent this 'Ambrose' from mounting the pulpit. But in the church 'over the way,' a son who did her no good would soon be shipped off to the Hottentots. He couldn't hurt the Hottentots, while he might create a considerable rumpus in the church."

"Now you men are always so hard upon clergymen," exclaimed tolerant Lady Angela. "Although you know I heartily condemn such narrow doctrine, I can't blame the man from preaching what certainly is a legitimate conclusion from the premise he lays down. Do be generous. He seems to be an earnest, albeit a harmless creature."

"Nobody honors the cloth more than I do, and nobody has more friends in the profession," replied Lawrence. "But this sermon only shows how many sides there are to the same subject. Looking at the sky from the bottom of a well, one would obtain a poor idea of its immensity."

Cyn. "St. Ambrose seems to be in the deepest kind of a well, then, to judge from the idea he gets of the heavens above him."

"Ah, poor boy," added Mr. Douce, "if his narrowness were food, he'd die before morning of hunger."

"He'd never do for Paradise," remarked Amelia.

"Never!" answered Lady Angela. "Neither Cousin Edith nor Annie would approve of it."

"I could preach better than that myself," said Cynicus, "if they would allow a ‘fellow’ to go up there without ‘taking orders.’"

"I have no doubt of that," laughingly replied Lady Angela, "for you are so mighty independent that you wouldn't take orders from anybody in *this* world."

"Unless from *you*, my lady," added Mr. Douce.

Miss Eunice Smart here joined the group, and began by saying, "Everything that young man said this morning was what might be termed ‘officially’ true; but the trouble was, he lacked judgment. He ought to have kept silent on some of those points. It is just as well," said she, "not to tell everything you believe all at once."

"Let it out gradually, you mean, perhaps," remarked Mr. Douce.

"Well, I mean, keep your own opinions to yourself, and preach about what everybody would agree to; it's much better."

"But Miss Eunice," answered Mr. Douce, "this gentleman's whole doctrine is so narrow that he would drive everybody away from the Church."

"No matter for that," replied Miss Smart, "the doctrine taught at Iota Seminary is pretty nearly what this young gentleman gave us to-day ; but I never saw a graduate from Iota who did n't know when to ' shut up.' "

" But do you believe in his *doctrine*, Miss Eunice ? "

" I believe, that carried to its logical conclusion, — which I don't think it ever need be, — but carried to its logical conclusion, one branch of the Church would ' bring up ' about where he ' came out ' this morning."

" But will you vote to call him to Paradise ? "

" Before I actually voted on the subject," answered Miss Smart, cautiously, " I would like to have an understanding with him on the ' filio-que ' question, and also on several minor points in the Revised Canons."

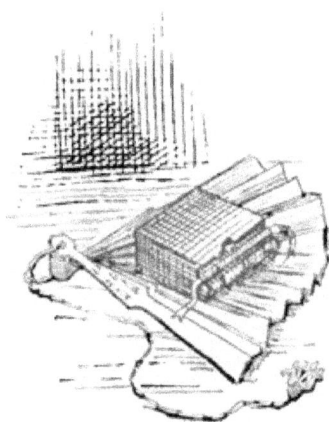

CHAPTER III.

DIFFERENT seasons of the year produce different
sensations: new life in spring, indolence in summer, accumulated strength in autumn, and sturdy
resistance in winter. This changing experience is
what toughens the fibre of northern races. It is
one of the many reasons why each season has its
lovers.

In " Paradise " the month of September is paradise indeed. This is the hazy month, and the
dreamy month, and the fruity month. It is the artists' month, and the tourists' month, and the invalids' month. Hearts are as big as melons then :
minds are as fruitful as apple-trees. The evenings
are so cool : the shadows are so long : the shawls
are so comfortable : the drives are so invigorating :

the roads are so brown, and what "he says" is so
lovely. The grapes have all been picked : the frogs
have formed themselves into solemn choruses ; the
screeching tree-toads are splitting their throats,
while all nature is thanking God as loud as ever it
can for the yellow harvests.

It was a great privilege to take one of Mr.
Worthington's easy-chairs and place it on the little
platform outside the hut on "Top-Knot" Hill of a
September afternoon. The view before one, which
goes rapidly downward and outward over the
placid landscape for twenty or thirty miles, has a
most quieting influence upon the beholder. The
blue horizon in the misty distance looks like the
ocean : while the little lake at the left, the red-
roofed railroad station at the right, the white
spire of the distant village, and even the serpen-
tine road, as it goes winding up the long incline
towards Jericho, complete a picture of quiet content.

There are all sorts of men in the world : some
are men of taste who love art and nature, and
women (who by the way combine them both).
There are others also whose prominent character-
istics are good sense and gentle manners. These
valuable citizens have a genial way of doing polite
things ; they do not expect you to thank them
more than one "good once," if they have done you
a favor : they differ from certain other brethren
who, if they happen to loan you a handkerchief to

supply the place of your own unfortunately left at home, are looking out all through life afterwards to see whether you are sufficiently grateful to them for this favor.

Mr. Worthington was not one of this sort. In July he gave strawberry-parties to the children; in September, among other courtesies, he regaled his older friends on " Top-Knot melons; " and it was a great honor to be an invited guest on such occasions.

There is an aroma about a cantaloupe melon which, heaven be praised, no chemist can imitate; and when that melon is icy cold, and perfectly ripe, whether one eats it with pepper and salt, with sugar, or with no condiment at all, he may be sure that he is partaking of something more delicious than Jupiter Olympus, with all his naughty luxuriousness, ever dreamed of.

One hazy afternoon in September, Mr. Worthington gave a melon party to some of his friends in Paradise.

This gentleman's guests looked like a moving mass of gay-colored exotics as they sauntered up the steep incline of " Top-Knot."

The host had fetched from the hut all his skins, rugs, and easy-chairs, and placed them at convenient spots over the grassy plateau, which were soon monopolized by an appreciative company.

Old " Lily-pad," the setter, lay at full length in the cool shadow, and there was nothing wanting to

make the party homogeneous. His friends did
what all friends do when they come together —
they talked.

"How about the new parson?" said Cynicus
Donce.

"They haven't got one?" inquired the interested Amelia.

"I believe nothing has actually been caught yet.

I wanted to hear if there was any bite?" said
Lawrence.

"Paradise won't be satisfied with *any* sort of
fish: she must have her pick of the assortment,"
spoke up Miss Brown, with a toss of the head.

"No 'small fry' for her, I trow," suggested Miss
Jones.

"You are right, my dear," said Lady Angela.
"Paradise needs a respectable, broad-minded gentleman; a good churchman, with an intelligent

wife, who can live on a very small salary and yet appear as contented as if he had all the luxuries of the season."

"Yes," rejoined Mr. Douce; "but he must be *unmarried*."

"That will never do," suggested Lawrence, "for he would be torn to pieces by his spinster parishioners."

"I don't fear that at all," replied Lady Angela. "But a married and experienced man would be more proper and respectable for such an old parish as Paradise; besides" —

"Now you will make a great mistake," interrupted Cynicus, "if you don't select a gentleman entirely free from any uxorial entanglements."

"It can't be," said Cousin Edith. "Amie and I would not feel willing to make such a dangerous unmarried experiment."

"Why!" continued Mr. Douce. "It is undeniable that celibacy increases the popularity of a popular preacher."

"I don't agree with you," said Lady Angela.

"How can you say so?" replied Mr. Douce. "Of two parsons with equal attractions of mind and manners, the unmarried one would be sure to 'carry the day' in the long run."

"Well, I don't see why he should," sighed Cousin Edith.

"Because," continued Mr. Douce, "the genus clergyman has ever been a subject of transcendent interest to the vast majority of women. They somehow feel as if he were composed of different ingredients from ordinary men. There is something so mysterious to them in the connection between wicked man and that which is pious and good, that he piques their curiosity."

"That may be the case with some women, but it is not so with me," said Miss Brown. "A clergyman to me is only an ordinary man hitched to a prayer-book."

"Still, I sometimes think," interrupted Amelia, "that we girls *do* consider ministers to be so blessed by heaven that they have no such feelings as other masculines have. The trouble is to know where so many bad traits go to so suddenly, and so many good ones come from, to occupy the vacancies."

"I can't believe, however," added Miss Jones, "that even clergymen are entirely free from all the temptations of the w., the f., and the d."

"To look at their placid faces and sweet expressions, no one would suspect they *ever* had any," murmured the pretty girl just from school.

"I rather think," said mine host in his kindliest manner, "that if the truth were told, a young, unmarried, and decent-looking clergyman has more young ladies in love with him than any other man in his parish. I don't think enough allowance is made for his sore temptations on the one hand, and his self-control on the other. I both envy and pity him."

"You need n't pity *him*," answered Cynicus Douce. "It is the young ladies of his parish who need your pity."

"*They* need my pity?"

"Yes: for, as I said before, they have the crudest and most extraordinary notions of a young minister. They seem to think that it is not possible for so religious a mortal ever to have any feeling of jealousy, hatred, or malice in his heart, like other sinners; that he never falls in love, unless according to the true biblical and patriarchal method; that he writes his love-letters from a sense of duty and a concordance; says grace every time he visits his lady-love, and 'offers himself' by quotations from the sacred writers."

Miss Brown laughed heartily at this nonsense, and exclaimed: "Only think of him reading the 'Commandments' every time he saluted his *fiancée!* No, Mr. Douce, a parson is something more than a walking collect with a white cravat, and something less than a saint perched on a blue rainbow."

"So he is to me," answered Mr. Douce. "I was merely describing how an unmarried clergyman sometimes impresses the average young lady of his parish; and viewing the question in this light, these gentlemen are placed in an entirely false position, for the circumstances of their office naturally make them the cynosure of all eyes, and thus help to place them in this unique yet popular situation.

It inclines me to believe the truth of that wicked saying, that there are three sexes in the world — men, women, and ministers."

"I don't know about the sex question," said Lawrence, laughing, "but I do believe there are only two sorts of ministers, as there are only two sorts of women in the world: those that are worth everything and those that are worth" —

"Friends!" interrupted Mr. Worthington, "our melons and peaches are awaiting our pleasure, — let us go into the hut and 'discuss' them at our leisure."

The fruit was delicious. Each succeeding melon was cooler and more aromatic than the preceding one; while peaches and cream, plum-cake, and a mysterious "something" else, peculiarly indigenous to "Top-Knot," completed the unique *menu* of the occasion.

When the cigars were brought in or rather "out" and lighted, the company moved once more to the green plateau, and from its airy height viewed the swiftly declining sun as he marched toward his bed of clouds.

Some of the party had but lately arrived from abroad, and conversation turned upon the changes which almost always occur during a long absence.

"That's the trouble with these protracted intervals," said Mr. Douce. "I always feel sad when my friends are 'packing up' for 'the grand tour,' because I know that when 'Eddy' has grown up, and 'Sadie' has acquired Sanscrit, while 'Maria's' projecting teeth have been made perpendicular, and her winking stopped, — 'the old folks at home' have all this time been sickening and dying, and losing their minds, 'Josiah' has been married, 'Ellen' engaged, the old horse has been killed, and 'Tommy Traddles' has gone to Texas."

"That's the worst of it," said Miss Brown; "in this age of telephone and phonograph, it hardly pays to shut one's eyes for fear that something wonderful will take place between the winks."

"Oh, dear!" said Amelia. "That is very true. People who are anxious for traveling forget that the things of this world are so nicely adjusted that one set cannot be jostled without disturbing all the rest."

"We are all like rows of bricks," answered Mr. Donce; "the tilting of one row tottles over the whole file directly in front of it."

"And our friendships go in the same way," said Miss Smith; "like modern mortar, there is no stick to them."

"What is that long procession coming up the hill?" cried out Amie. "There seems to be one man with a chair on his head, another with a feather-bed; and then comes a 'buckboard' piled up with things, and somebody walking behind with a sun-umbrella. It isn't a funeral, is it?"

Of course everybody sprang up to see the wonderful spectacle. Almost immediately, however, there was a great shout of laughter as the company discovered their delightful friend and sufferer, the Beautiful N. E., who was slowly approaching the feast at so late an hour.

"Run away and help her!" exclaimed Lady Angela, whereupon there was a general scamper to the ambulance.

The hospital cavalcade was composed of curious impedimenta. Thomas, the quiet man-servant, had on his head a certain particular chair belonging to his mistress, which just fitted the "right spot" of his mistress's back. Parker, the maid, carried under one arm a large pillow of eider-down, marked with a beautiful monogram "N. E." encircled by what appeared to be a necklace of quinine pills; while in the other she held over the head of the sufferer a silken parasol of delicate tea-rose color. It was "pinked" and "pantaleted" three rows deep, with an ivory handle of an unearthly tint.

The N. E. herself, poor child, lay on the "buckboard" at an angle of forty-five degrees, and was bolstered up on three large cushions, an elegant lap-robe, and little footstool. She wore a gown of exactly the same shade as her parasol. It was cut *à la princesse*, with a jabot of delicate lace and ribbon down the front, with a train of the same material. A cluster of "Jacqueminots" (just received from a friend in New York) completed the elegance and simplicity of her toilet. Her lisle-thread, clocked stockings were of the same delicate hue, and of Balbriggan manufacture.

The pure country air had already done wonders for her. The color of her cheeks eclipsed that of the rest of her attire, and, like any other masterly production, the eye was made to rest upon the strongest point, to which all other points were mere accessories. Her brownish, childish, wavy hair lay in undulating heaps over her brow; and as she alighted from the low buckboard, and sank into her eider-down dais, she resembled a beautiful rose-bud just fainting a little for want of water.

A score of sympathizing friends were quickly about her with peaches and cream, an eighth of a freshly cut melon, and quite a large slice of wedding-cake, to appease the cravings of exhausted nerves. With a graceful sweep of the hand, however, she stopped them by saying, "I never eat before I take my quinine. Won't you kindly get the pill-box from Thomas?"

The N. E.'s diction was superb. When she said "Won't you," she did n't say "woon-chew," as so many of us do, but pronounced each word separately. The "won't" had a "t" on it, and the "you" had a "u." It was pleasant to hear her converse.

"You see before you," said Mr. Worthington, grandiloquently, looking at the declining sun, "the great cosmopolite of the world. He is at home in all countries: has no prejudices; shines on the evil and the good, and goes straight to his couch regretted by an hemisphere."

"There is nothing mean about the sun," replied Mr. Lawrence, with his eyes fixed on the departing luminary. "If everybody would copy him, and mind his own business, we should all be the happier!"

"It is this interference which makes us all hate each other," said Mr. Douce. "It is surprising to find so many disagreeable people in the world whose prominent fault is not minding their own business."

"Why, Cynicus," exclaimed Miss Brown, with a laugh, "you're a miserable old pessimist, I'm afraid!"

"You're right, my friend," answered Cynicus; "everything you say convinces me of it. But have you never remarked how many disagreeable people there are?"

"We can't help seeing some, of course," replied Lady Angela, looking at him with a quizzical expression. "But why not notice the agreeable ones, too? I don't meet many disagreeable people.

Everybody seem to have something to recommend them — even pessimists."

"It may be dyspepsia." said Mr. Douce, " but it seems to me that agreeable people are only conspicuous by their rarity. Let me tell you what Habberton and I used to do when we were in college: We would start from the Campus and walk to the City Hall and back, and count the number of disagreeable people encountered on the way. One day we 'bagged' thirty-nine: and, as 'poor Artemus' would say, 'it wasn't a very good day for them, either.' Now thirty-nine in two miles is not so bad."

"What constitutes a disagreeable person?" inquired Miss Brown, fearing she might be one.

"There are twenty or thirty kinds." replied the pessimist. "Some have eternal smirks on their faces: some are always saying disagreeable things: some take your politeness to them for servility, and accordingly treat you with contempt: some pretend not to see you in the street when they *do* see you: some are forever 'harping' on small matters, and quarreling about it: some are always remarking upon what you *ought* to have done: some talk about you behind your back, and pretend they don't: some damn you with faint praise."

"Heavens!" exclaimed Amelia, "you've told us enough: and if you don't stop we'll put *you* in the category yourself."

"I haven't half got through, but I'll just go on

to say, that all these disagreeable people were confined in an invisible pen, and the most disagreeable
one of all we used to choose to 'keep the door;'
we found that we changed this keeper almost every
day."

The company laughed merrily at this, and said
that Mr. Douce was not half so bad as he pretended to be.

"Maybe not," said Douce. "I really don't think
I *am quite* such a wretch as you will probably say
the individual is who wrote this piece which I cut
from the last issue of 'The Home Circle.'"

"Let's hear it."　"Read it up," said many
voices.

"It is so rich," said Mr. Douce; "and such a
lie, that it becomes almost
ludicrous."

"What is the name of the
article?"

"The views of Archibald
Bald, after fifteen years' experience in our best society
— ten of them as a married
man, and the other five as a
nondescript."

Mr. Douce commenced to
read the article: —

"It sounds a little start-
ling to say that there are some human natures, in
what is called 'fashionable society,' devoid of the

sentiment of natural affection; but every day teaches us that this world is a conglomerate of many ingredients, and it is no longer wonderful that specimens of such characters are found. These individuals are confirmed egoists. They possess no active principle of love for their fellow-creatures. They are votaries of ambition and self-interest. They delight in the results of their cunning manipulation of society. Luckily for them, want of heart is seldom coupled with want of intelligence.

"It seems to be true that — within certain limits — the less the heart the more of a certain kind of talent. Things become abnormal only when there is either too much or too little of any necessary factor; so, in a worldly point of view, while it is true that too much heart causes its possessor disappointment, too little of it engenders stoicism and cruelty, — both being abnormal states of being.

"A person without any natural affection could never become an angel, while he might be well fitted to occupy the position of tyrant, or despot.

"It is fashionable to be heartless, because, somehow, heartlessness is coupled with success. The 'dimness' of snobbism is only a milk-and-water form of it. A merchant who has a heart is not generally the *richest* man in the community, although he may be the *happiest*.

"A landlord without a conscience generally collects more of the money due him, and is a much greater miser than he whose eye glistens at the sight of poverty. A man who gives thump for thump in the jostle of life, and rides rough-shod over society, is the one who has the best chance of exercising his skill in these particulars.

" According to the popular creed, success is life, non-success, death. To succeed, a man must be without a heart. To fail, he has only to possess one. The soul of trade is self-interest; therefore, the more the self-interest, the more the trade.

" Popular logic is very simple, and the deduction comes very easy. The result of all this is that love for others and self-sacrifice are seldom found in the mart of trade. Instead of these, 'tit for tat' and 'quid pro quo' jostle you at every turn.

" Society acknowledges all this, and admits that it is necessary to success; yet flatters itself that 'way down in its inmost heart there is, somewhere, an exhaustless philanthropy; and perhaps there is — I don't happen to see much of it.

" When we leave the mart of trade and ascend to the 'dress-circle' of society, we meet there a different species of the same tribe. At the door of this cultivated sphere everybody assumes a mask, which, once put on, is only laid away with death.

" Presenting to each other this false front, we are enabled to say to our dearest friend the very opposite from what we mean. We appear glad when we are sorry; we weep when we are really laughing, and we are gayest when we are saddest. Some

people call this 'conventionalism.' Whatever it is,
it engenders an unique species of humanity. This
society exotic numbers among its fraternity both
men and women. There are in 'society' no-hearted
mothers and no-hearted fathers, as there are no-
hearted saints and no-hearted sinners. Among the
motley group of this species, let us select a single
example.—'*ab uno disce omnes*.' I take the first
that comes to hand. It is a man. Now, why is it
that disappointment rises in the mind at this announcement? 'A no-hearted man!' says society.
'It goes without saying.' 'Would n't it be better,
and more entertaining, if search should be made
until, peradventure, a specimen of the other sex be
discovered?' Perhaps society is right. By dint of
great endeavor we have found such an one. There
she sits before us in all her majesty.

"This individual seems to have been born without the capacity of loving. Cool, calculating, and
sallow, she excites love in others, without a scintil-
lation of it in herself! She is a hunter who brings
down her game by adroitness. Sighings and tears
are not found in her vocabulary. Self-control sup-
plies the place of passion, and a sluggish circulation
of a throbbing pulse. She takes every possible advantage of her natural charms, in order to success.
She modulates her sharp voice to a persuasive key,
concealing its natural asperity with consummate
tact. Her life's secret — were it ever known — is
ambition. Her apparently pliant will is in reality

inflexible. In her association with men, she bids
for their devotion by every artifice at her command.
To every favoring breeze she sets her sails, — provided that it brings her to the haven "where she
would be," — success. To see a strong man surrender to her blandishments, and sit a vanquished
prisoner at her feet, is a 'sweet boon' which makes
her anthracite eyes to glisten. To obtain his love
and to gain the mastery of his opinions is her single
aim.

"If she has no thought of returning his affection,
it is because she actually has none to return. But
so cleverly does she simulate love, that her willing
vassal simpers at her feet, never quite, but always
'to be' blest. Never overcome by 'her feelings,'
she is pretty sure of doing the 'right thing' under
all circumstances.

"No solecism is ever laid at her door, and her
morals are, apparently, as correct as her manners.
She has several secret unwritten aims in life. One
is, to be considered the most beautiful woman in
society. If nature denies her that, then she bends
all her efforts to become the most fascinating. If
this is impossible, then the most fashionable, and so
on. The 'most something' she will be, even if it
is the most dangerous of her sex. Having achieved
success in some one of these directions, she is apt to
be patronizing to certain of her aspiring companions who have not been quite so fortunate. Such a
woman has a deal of tact, and finds it advantageous

to be attentive to the aged. 'It is not a bad thing, you know,' to hear these good people say of her, 'she is so kind and attentive.'

"Such a woman, also, is very particular in her social obligations. To strangers, if they happen to be guests of the best people, she is especially gracious. Of her poor relations she is not always quite so solicitous—for to such an one—who may perhaps have just successfully planted her foot on a certain coveted plane of social standing—what greater misfortune than to meet on the boulevard 'poor Aunt Rebecca,' or threadbare 'Uncle Josiah?'

"Her husband, poor man, was one of the few 'eligibles' who nibbled at her matrimonial hook when she first seated herself on the banks of life. The others—happy creatures—got away just in time to 'save their bacon,' leaving their sentimental rival fast entangled in the fatal net. This 'catch' was a rich one, and on it she has gloated ever since. Position and wealth is good diet for famished seekers, so the no-hearted wife is gorged and happy. She is most 'out of place' when she pays visits of condolence, and endeavors to sympathize with real sorrow. Here tragedy becomes comedy; and her words of pity are mere ghosts of sound. Nevertheless, no-hearted women are of some value after all, for they are the ones who never forget themselves. When the house is burning up, or when people are dying, they are perfectly self-possessed, and know just the right thing

to do.   By their thoughtfulness the silver is saved,
even though the baby burns up, and the grand
piano is safely moved into the neighboring lot, and
the bearers' gloves are just the right number.

"In domestic life, too, they often make good
mothers.   On this point — that of children — they
come nearer to an exhibition of affection than on
any other.   Yet there is no self-sacrifice in dressing
'little Maria,' and 'cunning Ethel,' so as to attract
attention and make people turn in the street and
say, 'Those are Mrs. Saintley's lovely children' —
'So like mamma' — 'Such a French accent!'   But
when she gets out on the avenue she is apt to over-
look other people's children, unless it possibly be
Lady Alice's, or those of Madame La Comtesse.

"The no-hearted woman snubs her husband
dreadfully.   Although he is strong enough to double
her up and throw her out of the window, she knows
by experience that he loves her too well to do anything of the kind.   So she discovers his little weaknesses, and plays upon them a delightful tune at
her pleasure.   First, she calls forth his admiration
and love by simulating unfeigned attachment, then
she tantalizes him by continual disappointment,
until, wound up in her toils, the warm-hearted
booby tumbles into the pit prepared for him by his
cool-headed Delilah.   In every-day life she takes
care to be just a little disagreeable and indifferent;
not doing her whole duty, and yet not wholly neg-
lecting it.   She is guilty of more sins of omission

than of commission, and so manages to sail over life's seas pretty smoothly; giving her husband a threadbare sort of happiness, and herself a good deal of selfish satisfaction. She dies a stoical old woman.

"One can scarcely associate domestic love with such an alliance. Of the two, the wife is much the better off, because her idea of joy is mere success, and this she has attained. It is difficult to say just what the other party got for his money. The best that can be affirmed is, that he bought a plated imitation of the real article.

"Even when a kind Providence takes pity on the husband and removes him from this pinchbeck happiness, it mysteriously seems to redound, even *then*, to his partner's gain; for there are instances where even this event has banished from her path the last stumbling-block to a wife's ambition.

"On this lugubrious occasion the subject of our remarks is tearless for weeks together. 'Stunned,' people say she is. Her crape is very deep, but very becoming. Her pale countenance exhibits the ravages of inward grief. Her cap is exquisitely plain, and of the latest mode. When the will is read and she hears that she is still to have twenty thousand dollars a year, and all the plate and the family lace, she folds her hands with a heavenly expression of resignation. At the proper time, however, after the weary months of etiquette have rolled away, she emerges from her tribulation with a very good appetite and a pair of huge solitaires."

After he had finished reading, Mr. Cynicus Douce folded up the slip and replaced it in his pocket-book.

"That's a libel on the sex!" said Amelia.

"It's a foul slander on woman, written by a coward!" bravely exclaimed Miss Brown.

"No such creature was ever born!" remarked Miss Jones.

"She's worse than Becky Sharpe!"

"The individual who wrote that was an opium-eater!" said Lucy.

"It doesn't make it true, ladies, because he says so," added Mr. Douce.

"He magnifies into perfected traits of character, what in nature are never more than bare suggestions," said Mr. Worthington.

"Yes," interrupted Mr. Douce, "we all undoubt-edly have two natures within us, and one of these natures has been diabolically magnified by the genial writer of this article beyond all bounds."

"Two natures!" said Miss Brown. "I believe we all have two, — at least I have, — and I'm con-stantly settling disputes between them. It's a great bore, this hot weather."

"Come, Douce," remarked Mr. Worthington, "as you have suggested this dual idea, why can't you give us your views on the subject *in extenso!*"

"It's too late," said Douce.

"I don't mean now. Write them out and read them at Paradise Hall. We'll all go, — fifty cents a head."

"All right," answered Mr. Douce, "I'll do it if you will promise to sit it out."

Of course they promised, and so it was agreed that Mr. Cynicus Douce should formally present his views on "our dual individuality" at Paradise Hall the next Wednesday evening at eight o'clock, for the benefit of the library fund.

The melon party then took leave of their hospitable host under the starlight.

CHAPTER IV.

THE LAST CHAPTER IN THE DIARY OF AN UNFORTUNATE GENTLEMAN.

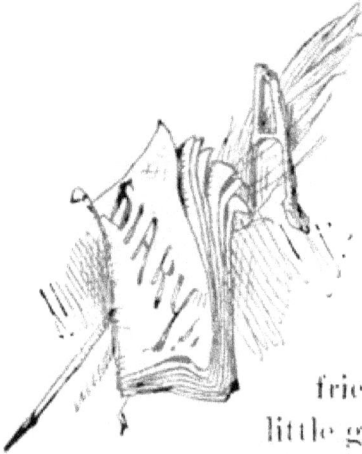

CCORDING to promise, Mr. Douce drew from his pocket the diary of the unfortunate gentleman, found in his chamber after his demise, and proceeded to read the last portions of it to his friends on the "Hill." The little group of attentive listeners gathered around him were eager to hear what else the poor creature had to say about himself and the cruel world which had used him so badly. The ladies of the company, remembering the merciless treatment which he had received at the hands of the "young person in Rome," as Mrs. George Madison Taggart called her, were filled with the hope that the concluding chapters of this doleful history would embody a happier tale, and unfold a better future for their deceased brother. Mindful of their own innocence of conduct toward the other sex, they condemned, without reserve, the heartless coquetry of Eleanor Donald. They vowed that if these concluding chapters did not exhibit something more noble and complimentary to their own sex, they would believe the whole thing was a trumped-up affair of Cynicus Douce's, and not at all the truthful tale it pretended to be.

"Ladies," began Mr. Douce, "please remember that this is a large world, and in it are people holding every shade of opinion, and influenced by every variety of motive. We must not deceive ourselves with the thought that real people are made up like the heroes and the heroines of modern romance. The real human heart is a common sort of an affair after all, and its action is governed a good deal after the simple rule of selfishness and self-preservation. We instinctively pursue that which will redound to our own advantage, and are too apt to be careless about what may happen to our neighbor. We seldom see those ideal men and women who strut across the stage of modern fiction, parading across our stage of experience; and so, I think, we would much better look at life just as we find it, than be always imagining it to be what it is not."

Mr. Douce stopped to breathe after this little virtuous speech, whereupon Amelia said : —

"For my part, every-day human nature is so hidcous that I love to imagine that I live in an atmosphere where things are what I would *like* to have them."

"Yes," replied Mr. Douce, "but the constant reading of the modern novel puts us in a false sphere; and this it is which unfits a man to cope with the ugly realities of life about him. Give me the truth, the immortal truth, bitter or sweet, *then* I know just where I am. No mawkish sentiment about what never was, will ever make it easier to earn my living."

"I agree with you," replied Lady Angela. "And it is this unreality, I take it, wherein lies the bad effect which modern romance produces upon us. But how beautifully we women *do* act in these works of fiction. I like to cheat myself with the belief that it's all true."

"No doubt you are all right, and all wrong, my friends," exclaimed Miss Brown. "Novels are mighty nice things, and I expect to read them all my life. But let's hear our deceased friend's last words first, and then we'll discuss this other question. Shall Mr. Douce begin?"

"He shall," they all said.

Here appeared on the green a servant with a pitcher of iced lemonade, with tumblers. The clinking ice gave a most refreshing sound. They all partook. After a bumper of this delicious beverage Mr. Douce read the title of this chapter, which was, —

"TOUJOURS — A SWISS IDYL.

FROM Strasbourg to Bâsle, from Bâsle to Neuchâtel, from Neuchâtel to Geneva, and from Geneva to Chamounix, — that was the route we took. After crossing the Tête-Noir as far as Martigny, we intended to drive round to Vevay ; then go to Berne, Thun, Interlachen, and Lauterbrunnen, so as to be ready to commence a pedestrian tour over the Bernese Alps. At Chamounix it rained like "everything," but when we reached Martigny the weather cleared again and promised to be steady. The next morning, after our arrival there, was superb, and we decided at once to ascend the Grand St. Bernard and lodge for a night at the Hospice. The journey up the pass, as far as the little village of Liddes, is performed in *chars-a-bancs*. Then, after the noon-day meal, the mules are taken from the vehicles and mounted for the rest of the way, some twelve miles, to the Hospice.

" As we ascended from the vale of Martigny by the little winding road which carried us past the rustic chalets, the low cow-stables, the gushing streams of water, and the sturdy villagers, we had full opportunity to enjoy the scene. Clouds hung over the misty mountain tops, then cleared away, leaving their icy summits in bold accentuation against the bluest sky.

"Wreathing, lazy smoke found its way into the upper air; bleating goats and tinkling cow-bells sounded in the distance; while groups of peasants in rough homespun stockings and hob-nailed shoes moved by our carriage on their way to and from the hills above.

"At breakfast we had partaken heartily of the aromatic Swiss honey, which, with fresh bread and butter, is never more palatable than when one leaves the vale of Martigny for the Alps above him. As we mounted higher and higher we observed a party of tourists at some distance in advance, which was apparently bound for the same destination as ourselves. Some curiosity was naturally excited to discover who and what they were. On nearer inspection their dress and general appearance proclaimed them to be English. Two young girls, two young men, and a more elderly couple, who might be man and wife. We learned all this from observation from our *char-a-banc*, as the cavalcade wound its way around the big bowlders and across the mountain torrents.

"Sitting in a constrained position hour after hour was so fatiguing that I alighted from the "char" for a walk. A powerful mule hauled our carriage, and I could but notice her black points and fine action. She drew us up the mountain with great ease, showing no signs of distress, while her bright eyes glanced from right to left, and her delicate ears moved backward and forward.

"When she stopped to catch breath, I noticed that our Jehu fed her with bits of black bread which he cut from a loaf taken out of his box. Then, after patting the animal, we would start cheerily up again toward Liddes.

"I soon caught up with the English party, with their alpen-stocks and their green veils, their red 'Murrays' and their healthy faces.

"As we sauntered up the winding pass I found the men of the company, with whom we fell into conversation, pleasant and chatty. I spied a couple of Alpine roses just by the road-side, which I gathered and courteously presented to the young girls, who accepted them with the usual 'thanks.' Farther on I saw, under an immense jutting bowlder, and down some distance from our line of direction, a small bunch of edelweiss, which I sprang forward to pick. This interested the whole company

a good deal, who stopped and watched my move-
ments with curiosity. I managed at last to seize
upon it, at some
little risk, per-
haps, of falling
off the precipice,
yet not enough
to make it of
any moment. I
brought the cov-
eted white flow-
ers to the expect-
ant group and
gave them, with
a decent show of gal-
lantry, to the fairest of
the two girls. This per-
son deserves especial no-
tice, because she proved to be
a perfectly charming and delightful woman. What author is it
who has said, ' The most beautiful,
the most lovable, and the purest
form in which nature ever exhibits
herself, is in a young woman under
twenty; well bred, well born, and well educated;
with hair like a fairy and head like a goddess;
straight, lithe, and pure-hearted; with shell-like
ears and chiseled nose. Her laugh like running
water, and her breath a morning zephyr. Her

clear, guileless eyes look at you with innocence, while, like the wild game in an unexplored country, she walks about her enemy, man, without fear or tremor?' The above description fitted the object of our notice in many of its details. She must have been, however, one-and-twenty at least, while her hair, instead of resembling a fairy's, was straighter and more self-contained than is generally attributed to those creatures of fancy. In other particulars she satisfied the above requirements. As we walked along, we compared each other's alpen-stocks, and the names of the various Swiss wonders branded upon them. It turned out that her party was about leaving Switzerland, having gone over much the same road upon which we were preparing to enter. She told me that they had just passed a night on the ' Faulthorn,' and she maintained that its summit was much higher than the top of the pass we were now mounting. Some of her party — her cousins and aunt — held the contrary opinion : and she immediately bespoke my partisanship to her side of the question. I told her that I had no doubt that she was correct in her supposition, as I happened to know that there was some eighty or ninety feet in favor of her mountain. Just then, as we rounded a corner, the cluster of unpainted chalets — composing the village of Liddes — came into view, and the whole company pressed eagerly forward towards it.

" The mules were unharnessed and hitched in

the shade, while the party amused itself as best it
could, awaiting the noon-day meal, which was being
prepared.

"I walked round to the log-stable to see the animals. There I found the driver of our *char-a-banc*
talking with the ladies of the English party, who
were admiring the mule which had pulled our carriage. The man cut off pieces of bread and held

them before the animal, which would prick up its
ears and advance towards the tempting morsel,
in quite a noble style.

"'What is its name?' asked the elder of the two
ladies.

"'Toujours, madame!' replied the driver, touch-
ing his visor.

"'Toujours! What an odd name. May I ask
why it has such a curious one?'

"'Oh, yes, certainly, madame!   We call her
Toujours because she is always so willing to go,
and always so good-natured, and always so hungry.'

"'I'm sure, then, Toujours is very appropriate
to her,' said the lady.

"'That is the best mule in the whole canton,
madame; and would n't mademoiselle sketch her
for my wife?' asked the man, looking towards the
younger lady.

"'I hardly feel up to that sort of thing,' replied the beautiful girl: — 'perhaps this gentleman
would,' looking at me as she spoke.

"'I don't mind trying,' said I, 'but let me get
a good look at her first,' and I walked around the
animal to examine her points. Soon after this I
entered what, by the sign over the door, was the
tap-room of the rude inn which served for a refuge
for travelers. I seated myself on a bench and before
a wide, long deal table which extended down the
whole length of the low-studded and vacant apartment, and upon which meals were served. I took
out my utensils for drawing, and commenced a
sketch of Toujours from memory.

"I drew her head and rubbed it out, then commenced again, got her expression, went on, came
to her fore-legs, and stopped to decide what was
best next to do, when I perceived what seemed to
be the quiet, regular breathing of something or
somebody just over my head. I raised my pencil

from the paper, and, while the color mounted in
my cheeks, I turned slowly about in the direction
of the sound. There, just above my shoulders and
not a yard from my own face, stood the beautiful
English girl and her aunt watching my operations
with respectful interest.

"'Excuse us for interrupting you?' said the
older lady, — 'but we are very much interested to
see how 'Toujours comes on.'

"'It is no interruption,' said I. 'I don't think
I've succeeded any too well.'

"'The likeness is very good; and how rapidly
you do it! You are something of an artist, I see.'

"'Yes, perhaps so. I am very fond of sketching,'
I replied, as I finished the drawing.

"'Oh, that is fine!' exclaimed the beautiful girl,
who had not spoken before, but who could not re-

strain the expression of her approval. 'It's capital, and so like Toujours. — please let me look at it.' — so she took the sketch in her own fair hands while I peeped just over her shoulder.

" This was the second step in our acquaintance; so when we started from Liddes for the Hospice, I felt that perhaps I was warranted in trotting beside her on Toujours for the remainder of the journey.

" The summit of the Grand St. Bernard is a gloomy spot : but very like all other summits of the Alps. The mere débris of the world — as if Omnipotence had piled up the pieces there, after finishing creation.

" Our united parties straggled up single file, to a barn-looking structure, and were met by one of the holy brethren, who at once dashed to the ground all my preconceived notions of the monks of St. Bernard.

" Instead of an aged man with cowl and sandal, with lantern and alpen-stock, followed by a faithful dog, we were received by a bustling young gentleman in glasses. He wore a tall black visorless hat, long garment, reaching to the feet, of the same material, and the white badge of his order about his neck. He was neither emaciated by penury, nor bronzed by exposure, but in the most affable manner he conducted us to the salon, where the cloth was laid for dinner, and he directed our attention to an open piano.

"A regular *menu*, with Bordeaux wine, took the place of the ideal fare of the monks of old. After this, the stranger's book was brought in for our signatures.

"The nationality of our newly made acquaintances was a certainty, in our minds, while they were not as well informed in regard to our own. For while we talked English perfectly well, we certainly were not English. And as there were so many blue-eyed Germans and Russian tourists who spoke the Anglo tongue without an accent, a well-bred curiosity was pardonable to discover whom we should actually prove to be. How well I remember the signatures of our English friends. That of my particular acquaintance was bold and very legible. She took the pen and wrote, 'Miss Edith Grey, Tamworth, England,' without hesitation. It then came to our own turn, and I noticed the look of suppressed satisfaction when they finally settled the question as to who and what we were. Such a merry time we had after dinner, singing national songs, and telling our adventures!

"The accommodations for the night at the Hospiece were abundant. The beds had canopies, albeit there was but one small window in our chambers, and that one cross-barred with iron.

" The next morning we awoke in a great snow-storm, and the look outside was anything but pro-

pitious. We attended early mass, deposited in the charity-box what we judged equivalent to a night's lodging, inspected the morgue, where were the unreclaimed bodies of those unfortunates who are found on the mountains, and then prepared our-selves to descend into the valley. The whole Alp was enveloped in a snow-cloud. We could scarcely

11

see our way, so that I feared lest Miss Grey might lose her self-possession and something befall her. This was my excuse for posting myself at her bridle, and guiding her mule down the blind and slippery pass.

"The party would at one time be completely lost in the great surging cloud; and then emerge again with weird effect from the enormous rifts which lay about us. This circumstance brought Miss Grey and myself constantly together, and I rejoiced that the snow was as thick as it was, and that I had the good fortune of being up in the clouds with such a charming woman.

"I shall not soon forget the grand sight of the lower valley, reveling in sunshine, and sparkling in the drops of the recent showers, which suddenly burst upon us, as we slowly emerged from the snow-cloud; first our feet, then our persons, and last of all our drenched and dripping heads. It was like a sudden revelation — a beautiful vision brought before our eyes.

"Weary, delighted, and filled with satisfaction, my companion and I bade our friends good-night at the foot of the mountain, promising to meet them all again on the following day. Unluckily, we were lodged at different hotels, which made it a little more difficult to meet; still that fact stimulated my wish to do so all the more. Some unfortunate experiences in former years had made me somewhat wary of placing implicit faith in anybody; yet I was strongly impressed that the sweet friend whom I had so recently met was true and noble.

"Another beautiful day had tempted the whole English party, with the exception of Miss Edith Grey, to make an excursion to a famous waterfall on the road to Vevay. Calling at their hotel after breakfast, and on entering their salon, I was graciously received by my new acquaintance, who begged me to select the easiest seat I could find, and told me that the rest of her party were away for a day's frolic. After consultation with a pleasant-looking Swiss courier, who had been their guide all through the mountains, she seated herself in my neighborhood, and beside a white porcelain stove.

"Every one who has traveled knows how easily people become intimate with others whom they chance to meet on their journey, and that one's most cherished friends are sometimes those whose acquaintance has been made in just this manner.

"'Did n't we have a charming day at the Hospice yesterday?' said my companion.

"'Indeed, yes, and unexpectedly so,' I replied, 'because I commenced the excursion as a matter of duty. I promised my friends at home to go there.'

"'I'm so glad that our last impressions of Switzerland are so delightful; and when we get back to England we shall all think that a monk's life on St. Bernard is not so bad a lot after all.'

"'When do you start for Paris?' inquired I.

"'To-morrow afternoon, I believe: and don't forget that when you come to England you must surely visit Tamworth.'

"'I could scarcely help doing so,' I answered; 'for to me, England *is* Tamworth, and Tamworth, England.'

"'I'm sure you would like it; and when you come to us, you must sketch my little filly that I ride on. But before I forget it, *would* it be asking too much for a sketch of Toujours? — "dear Toujours?" She was such a beauty.'

"'With the greatest pleasure in the world,' said I. 'Have you pencil and paper?'

"'Here they all are, so you've no excuse,' exclaimed she with a merry laugh. 'The pencil is lovely and sharp, is n't it? I did that.'

"'Just right; but what shall I draw upon?'

"'Here's the back of my music-book; will that do?'

"'The very thing.' What shall she be doing?'

"'Let me see. I think I'd like to have her hitched at the log-barn, when the driver fed her with bread, and you — were — just coming — no, just hitched at the barn, I think, will do.'

"'Yes! I know.'

"So I commenced the sketch, while a delicious repose fell upon the scene. As I drew, she looked over my shoulder, and rested her head on the back of my chair, and I could feel her sweet breath fan my cheek as it came and went; and sometimes, when I would stop drawing, and lean back in order to see the 'effect' of the sketch, my face would come 'mighty near' her own rosy countenance, but not a bit too near, and she did n't seem to mind it, and I know *I* did n't.

"It took me a long time to complete the likeness of Toujours; I don't think I ever was so long making one before, but I could n't bear to alter a single circumstance in the situation of things about us. Had I finished the sketch before I actually *did*, then it would hardly have been 'the thing' to sit *that* way any more, and my delight would have come suddenly to an end. Miss Grey said she must take the sketch in her own hands, to see it; and then I had to take it in mine, — 'just to alter something wrong about the ears of Toujours, — and then she must needs look at it herself again, 'to see if what I had done had improved it at all;' and then I wanted to take it 'just a second,' to 'rub out a wrong line about the fore-legs;' and then she said that I 'must let her have it, for I would certainly spoil it to touch it any more, — it was just perfect as it was.' And so we kept it up, from out of her hands into mine, until at last we had both the sketch and our hands in each other's hands, without realizing exactly what we were both about; and yet I think we both realized, 'a little,' the true position of affairs, after all.

"'That's glorious!' exclaimed my companion, after I had completed the picture for the fifteenth time: 'how can you do it so rapidly?' Now, I'll just pin it up here on the wall to show to Aunt Mary and my cousins when they return. You're very good, I'm sure,' she continued.

"'Not good,' said I, looking her in the eye, 'but happy.'

"'Has n't your talent for drawing given you much pleasure?'

"'Yes: and some queer adventures as well.'

"'Ah! do tell me some,' said she, in a pleading tone.

"'Perhaps I will, for I'm already commencing to feel communicative. It should be a reciprocal sort of an agreement, however.'

"'How queer that we should know each other so well away off here in Switzerland, when, day before yesterday neither of us suspected there was such a creature living,' said Miss Grey, with an expression of wonderment on her handsome face.

"'Yes, strange enough. I believe I was born just for this afternoon!'

"'I'm curious to know if you have parents,' she said, with elevated eyebrows and sympathetic voice.

"'No.'

"'A real orphan? How I pity you.'

"'Yes, a real, living orphan.'

"'Is that the reason why you look so sad?'

"'*One* reason.'

"'Do tell me about yourself. An orphan's experience must be very unique!'"

"'I 'll agree to relate an adventure which happened to me once while I was sketching away up in the hill-country of England, but only on one condition.'

"'And that one, of course'—said she (smelling an Alpine rose).

"'Is that you take pity on my motherless state, and confide something to me in return.'

"'Can an orphan be trusted?' inquired she, with a sweet smile.

"'Trusted! Don't you see, an orphan has nobody to whom it can possibly impart its secrets.'

"'I never thought of that before. I have a mind,' she added, after a moment's musing. 'I have a mind, if you 'll tell no one, and care to return to our hotel after luncheon, and will not ask too many questions, to narrate the circumstances of a case which happened to a young lady once—who was much younger than she is now—and who was wayward and foolish, and who would never do such a thing again as long as she lived.'

"'I promise, solemnly, on the word of an orphan.'

"'I know I ought n't to do it,' said she, pondering over the idea : 'but I just *must*, this once; and to an orphan, too, it really makes some difference, does n't it?' she inquired with winsomeness.

"'All the difference in the world,' cried I, as I bade her good-morning for the present, and rushed to my hotel for luncheon.

" After my return I found Miss Grey quite eager to listen to my adventure, for she seated herself at my feet, and raising up her full, brown gazelle eyes to mine, said, ' Begin immediately, for I am dying to hear it.'

"THE STORY OF A LEAD PENCIL.

" I was once passing the Sunday at a hotel in the lake and hill country of England, and in the neighborhood of a shining river. The little inn had quite a wide veranda in the rear, which afforded a splendid view of the distant water and the pretty village beneath us. The weather was warm, and the house was full of strangers. Among other parties I noticed one in particular, which consisted of two young ladies, and another older one who was their chaperon, and two male companions — students they appeared to be — who were evidently dear acquaintances, while one of these gentlemen was undoubtedly a lover of the younger girl. The boy was just at that stage of the passion when he had surrendered unconditionally to the enemy, and with all thought of further resistance abandoned was begging that he might simply wear her chains, and be put to the most

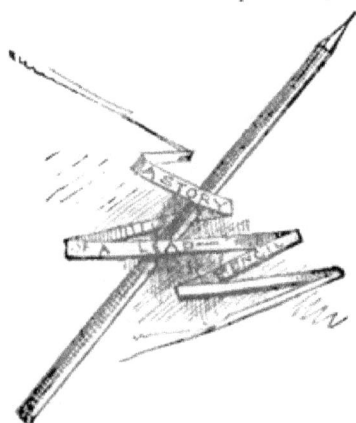

menial service, so that she be the gainer by it.
Poor fellow! I pitied him, and it was painful to
view his pale, passionate, and imploring attitude as
he approached his conqueror. She was like a beautiful kitten who had caught her first mouse. Her
great eyes sparkled with a laughing ferocity. Her
cheeks were burning with the flush of youth and
victory; while her lithe and girlish figure moved
about with the dignity and consciousness of a successful victor. There is no grander sight, in its
way, than a young girl's return from her first successful foray into an enemy's country; and this
one was a fair exhibition of such an event. She
glanced at her victim with delight, — first snubbing
him almost to tears, — then beaming upon him
with a look of such ineffable tenderness that it
made the young man tremble with emotion. Then
she would walk with him on the piazza, up and
down, up and down; 'cutting' her eyes about from
right to left, as if in search of other conquests;
taking care, however, to keep firm hold on the
writhing victim in her grasp.

"I noticed all this philandering as I sat in one
corner of the piazza, sketching a large oak, half
detached from the ground, and inclined over the
precipice, but still held firm by its roots to the soil.
The murderous purpose, then and there, entered
into my mind to try the power of my pencil, and
see if I could not attract the attention of the
beauty, madden with jealousy her boyish lover, and

finally steal an acquaintance with this beautiful
and untamed 'Katharine.' This is the way I went
to work : I sharpened my pencil, took a fresh sheet
of paper, and every time the little beauty approached my position on the piazza, I would look
at her so seriously, so admiringly, and so interest-
edly, that it at last attracted her attention. Then,
as she got close to where I sat, I would immediately
put down my head and commence to draw as rapidly as possible. After several repetitions of this
sort of pantomime, her curiosity was so piqued that
she could not restrain herself from casting sidelong
glances at the picture, as she moved up and down
the veranda. These glances became bolder and
bolder, until she became certain that it was her
likeness I was attempting to sketch.

"Now you must remember that this young lady
was still an imprudent and wayward school-girl;
that she was untamed as a colt, and, moreover, not
above seventeen years of age. She had already
conquered one manly 'booby' who was 'blubber-
ing' at her side, and was now seeking further to
satisfy her appetite with more dangerous game.
She looked beautiful as she proudly sailed by with
her languishing 'tender' beside her. He, wretched
boy, was already black with jealousy, and scowled
at me with direful vengeance as he passed by my
corner. Matters were fast approaching a crisis.
I said to myself, 'There is nothing gained by delay.
I certainly have a right to sketch with my pencil,

and if rocks and trees, why not pretty girls?'
Echo answered, 'why not?' So my mind was at
ease. Luckily at this juncture the rest of her
party appeared at the hall door with shawl and
parasol, all prepared for a walk to a neighboring
summit to witness the sunset. They asked the
beauteous 'Katharine' to accompany them. But
she excused herself on the score of a headache.
The chaperon then begged her, but she refused
again, alleging a desire to take a nap. The student
belonging to Katharine's companion next lent his
voice of entreaty, but she put him off with a pretty
laugh of derision. Finally, as a last resort, the
fainting lover ventured, *sotto voce*, and timidly, to
beseech her himself: 'For my sake, Kate,' said he;
but she ruthlessly snubbed him, in that loveliest of
all womanly ways, by ignoring his suggestion altogether, and saying, 'Now you all go and have a good
time, and when you return I shall be so bright from
my nap you won't know me. There, Maggie, take
my hat. It's broader-brimmed than yours, and
will keep the sun off better. Good-by!'

"So they were forced to go without her, lover
and all; leaving behind them the charming Kate
on a secluded piazza, a Sunday afternoon among
the mountains, and an artist somewhere in the distance, sketching her portrait,—a dangerous concatenation of circumstances, surely!

"A denouement was rapidly approaching. 'Katharine' stopped at the upper end of the veranda,

and leaning her pretty head on both her plump white hands, surveyed the wide, woody landscape which lay before her with anxious eye. Said I to myself, 'Will she now go in and leave me, or will she — Macawber-like — wait for "something to turn up."' One moment passed, then another, still another, with no change in the situation. 'By Jove! she's not going,' said I. 'What an opportunity! Everybody either in bed or on the top of a distant hill. I'll,— I've a good mind to perk up and show her her portrait! And if she remains where she is until I've counted ten, by Jove! I'll go — and — yes, I'll go and speak to her, whatever happens. One, two, three, four, five, six, seven, eight, nine, ten. Here goes!'

"As I finished counting, I arose from my place in the corner as quietly as possible, took the sketch in my hand, and walked in an easy, nonchalant manner toward the blushing maiden, who appeared to be so unconsciously beholding the crimson sunset.

"My hat was off a long way before I reached her proximity; and then, after swallowing rapidly several times, to enable me to do what I had never done in my life before, I spoke to the lovely creature without being properly presented.

"'I trust you will pardon my speaking without introduction, for I confess I was unable to resist taking a sketch of your face; and here it is in my hands to prove what I say.'

"'Oh, not at all, sir,' replied the young girl, frightened at the scene she had so rashly provoked.

"'Will you be pleased to look at it?' I continued, 'and see if it is like?'

"'Oh, thanks! I knew — I think I should recognize it anywhere. You have flattered me, sir!'

"'I don't think I have. I was attracted by your marvelous resemblance to a dear friend of mine. Will you honor me by accepting the sketch?'

"'Oh, thanks, sir! If you please I'd like to send it home.'

"'But I don't want you to send it home. I wish you to keep it.'

"'I will, then, and hang it in my dormitory!'

"'Ah, you are a school-girl, are you?'

"'Yes. I go to boarding-school; but this is my last term.'

"'And then' — said I.

"'Then' — said she.

"'And then — what, please?' I persisted.

"'I shall "come out," I suppose.'

"'Are you anxious to "come out," as you call it?'

"She looked at me with a knowing smile, and gave two or three quick nods of assent. I ventured to remark, —

"'When you *do* "come out," you'll have to be awfully "proper."'

"'I know it; and that is why I am having such a good time now.'

"'You are certainly having everything your own way up here, with *some* members of your party.'

"She eyed me askance for a moment, and while a deep color mantled her peachy cheek, replied, 'Oh, *he's* nothing!'

"'Won't you take a bit of a walk with me?' said I, beseechingly.

"'I told *them* I was going to take a nap,' she answered.

"'No matter,' cried I, '*they're* gone, and you are far from sleepy. Will you, please?'

"'Only once or twice, then, up and down the piazza,' she replied, as she straightened up from her leaning position on the balustrade, and wrapped her mantilla about her rounded shoulders.

"'I'm very grateful for "once or twice."'

"So we started on our tramp. That 'once or twice' was prolonged to hundreds and thousands. I found her as communicative as a little parrot. She imparted to me lots of family history; how this poor student had actually 'offered himself,' and how she was only having a harmless flirtation with him — 'nothing more;' that she couldn't think of 'marrying him,' or anybody, for three or four years at least, and that she really loved her cousin Joe better than all the world.

"'Couldn't you ever love anybody *but* cousin Joe?'

"'I might *play love*, but I don't think I could ever love that kind where you cry, and have to go and tell your mother all about it,' she answered, with an innocent expression on her pretty face.

"'Could you *almost* love anybody besides cousin Joe?'

"'Perhaps I might, a very little "almost."' said she, with a quizzical, coquettish expression which revealed the whole case to me ; so I added, —

"'I don't want you to forget me.'

"'I never shall,' she whispered.

"'I never can *you*,' I murmured, with deep feeling.

"'Nonsense! When you bid good-by, you'll never think of me again !'

"'When I leave you, it will be with painful emotions.'

" ' That 's splendid,' said she.

" ' When I go back to school, your sketch will always bring back the pleasantest memories. I 'll plague the girls awfully.'

" ' Thank you, very much! I would n't mind a little of that sort of thing.'

" ' I know I ought n't to talk with you in this way,' she said, with an expression of apparent sadness.

" ' If you do nothing worse than this, you will surely go to heaven.'

" ' It seems as if everything I want to do is always wrong!'

" ' Why, my little friend, your conscience is as tender as all the other angels'! You are doing nothing wrong — and won't you give me something to remember this afternoon by?'

" ' What *can* you want.'

" ' Oh, your glove, that bit of silk there — any little "snip" that I can keep.'

" ' You don't *really* want that!'

" ' Indeed, I *do*.'

" ' How much?'

" ' Ever and ever so —'

" ' Well! I really think you deserve some return for your — my likeness, and I 'll just give you this bow here, if you want it "ever and ever so," ' — she rattled on thus while she was detaching the scrap of ribbon from her dress.

" ' Allow me to help you!' said I.

" ' No! thanks! I can do it perfectly well myself; there — take it ' — (at this moment her party appeared returning from their excursion) — quick — quick. Oh, dear! There they all are, returning from their walk, and I have n't taken a nap after all; and they see me, and I 've told a lie, and there 'll be a pretty row. Run away as quickly as you can. What can I say? How shall I explain?' While she was giving vent to these expressions I stood silently by her side, holding the ribbon in my fingers and awaiting the impending shock.

"The party had indeed returned. The foremost one had already appeared at the door which opened on the piazza, and saw me plainly receive from her tiny hands the silken memento. This individual was the love-sick student. While the rest of her party crowded about Katharine, this young gentleman walked up to where I was standing and with anything but a saintly expression of countenance said : —

" ' I demand that you give up to me the ribbon which that young lady just gave you!'

" ' Who are you — and by what authority do you make such an extraordinary request?' I replied.

" ' I am that young lady's friend, and *that* is my authority,' said he, with a face blanched with anger.

" ' I am that young lady's friend also, and that is my authority for refusing your impudent demand.'

" Meanwhile, Katharine's party had retired with

12

her into the hotel — evidently in a troubled and disorganized condition, which left the young student and myself alone together.

"'You had no right, sir, to take advantage of the absence of her protectors, and accost that young lady without presentation, and if you communicate with her in any way again, you will have to account personally to me for your ungentlemanly conduct.'

"'My young friend,' said I. 'I admire your spirit and all that, but I can assure you that your charming friend has been in no way compromised by any act of mine; and I am proud to say that we are the very best of friends.'

"'You are a rascal,' said he; 'and I'll teach you better manners! Take that, for your artistic impudence!' With this ejaculation he struck at me with his fist. I easily eluded the blow, however, and catching him by the throat pinned him against one of the pillars of the piazza.

"'Ah! my boy; do you know that I can choke you to death, and throw your body over the cliffs, and *will* do so, too, if you don't listen to reason and my explanation.' Holding him there, I then went on: 'I don't want your girl, nor have I done anything to call forth all this rumpus. I merely showed your friend the little likeness which I had drawn of her, and then naturally fell into an agreeable conversation about it, which, by her sweet condescension and my own importunity, has lasted as long as it did. I can assure you that she has proved herself the most delightful of young ladies; that her manners are only equaled by her beauty, and that, in short, all the fol-de-rol which you are making about this little adventure is pure nonsense. Finally, I beg your pardon, sir, and the pardon of all your party, and the young lady's pardon too,

if I have done the least thing to offend any of them by my actions this afternoon.'

"During this long explanation I held the love-sick student firmly braced back against the post, but gradually eased the grip on his neck, as I approached the conclusion of my harangue. This afforded him great relief, and permitted him at last to ejaculate : 'I see — that — I was — mistaken, sir, and I accept your apology — and will go and make it all right with my lady-friend. Thank you,' he added, as I let go his throat and offered him a cigar. He didn't accept it, however, but vanished inside the hotel, leaving me in possession of the field and the little ribbon, which was well worth all the effort I had put forth to obtain it.

" Late that night, as I descended the main stair-way, I heard, far above me in the darkness, a sweet voice which whispered, 'Good-night and good-by, forever.' I looked up in the black air, but could see nobody : — and this was the end of the story of 'The Lead Pencil.''

" During the relation of this youthful episode Miss Edith Grey looked steadily up into my face, while a ruddy cheek told plainly that she had followed with interest every word of the narration.

" That night as we both sat together in the little inn at Martigny, while the gloaming stole silently over the vale, I confess to a deep feeling of contentment and delight, such as had seldom fallen to my lot before.

" ' You were very naughty to "carry on" so with the little lassie,' said Miss Grey, at last.

" ' It was my pencil that did it — not I.'

" ' Aren't you sorry that your pencil acted so naughty ?'

" ' I'm very sorry that I'm *not* sorry; but I'm not !'

"'You couldn't surely blame the lover for his indignation at your conduct?'

"'Not a bit: I admired his pluck.'

"'And you think you were very bold and wicked in accosting the little thing without an introduction: don't you?'

"'I suppose I must have been: but I'll never do it again!'

"'You were a very bad boy: but, to be frank with you, I believe I should have done the same thing, were I in your place.'

"'Had you been in the young girl's place, I should never have had the courage to do what I did.'

"'Why, I thought you were very courageous!'

"'Before angels! I never am.'

"'You must n't flatter me, for that 's not nice!'

"'Lead me not into temptation, then,' said I. 'And now we 'll have *your* little story, if you please.'

"'It 's getting too late for that, I see,—almost six o'clock. I fear we must defer it until we all meet in Tamworth.'

"'O Miserie! I'm truly disappointed,' said I, crestfallen, 'for I'm a first-rate listener!'

"'Then you would make a good father confessor,' she archly added.

"'To be the depository of *your* confession, I'd take orders this very minute!'

"'I would n't like you to be a priest, though!'

"'Why? Not long enough to hear your story?'

" ' A woman's confession is a tale of weakness, you know !'

" ' And of love ? Are they not equivalent terms ?'

" ' Perhaps so ! It is a wretched state, that of a mortal who has a secret which he can't impart !'

" ' Or *she* can't impart.' said I. ' They tell me that a woman's secret burns to gain utterance. She *must* tell it to somebody.'

" ' I 'll tell it all to *you*, in Tamworth.' said she, ' some day.'

" ' If I remain much longer, *I'll* tell all my secret to *you* here in this very inn.' replied I, with excitement.

" ' The hours have surely sped rapidly away today.' she seemed to think aloud.

" ' Yes. How swiftly falls the foot of Time which only treads on flowers.' quoting the old trite line.

" ' Dear me, we all go back to England to-morrow by the diligence.' said Miss Edith Grey, with a sigh.

" ' Ah, how unfortunate ! At what o'clock ?'

" ' Eleven, I believe.'

" ' I shall certainly be here to see you off : and you will pardon me, I know.' said I, quietly. ' if I confess how greatly I regret your departure. This day has been to me a day of heavenly peace.'

" ' Do you, indeed, regret our going ? Well, I have no hesitation to acknowledge that the agreeable events clustering about our newly-made acquaintance and this little quiet evening at Martigny make it equally sad for me to say good-by.' Here the red sun sank behind the snow-capped peaks. We took each other's hands and bade farewell, and then farewell again, and yet another farewell before I realized what I was doing, or could tear myself from her dear presence. I returned at last to my hotel with a throbbing heart, and, if I must confess it, a tearful eye.

"The next morning I hastened to see the party off. 'Mine host,' at the inn, told me that the last night's mail had brought dreadful news to the English party. The father of one of the young ladies had suddenly died, and the whole company had rushed away back over the Tête-Noir to Chamounix, and so on as rapidly as possible toward England.

"Here I was then, suddenly separated by a cruel fate from one in whom I had learned to confide, and to whom I was just about to open my heart; from one also with whom I felt perfectly *en rapport*, and who was fast growing to be a dear object of my regard. What was I to do? Where was I to go? In this case there was no deceit, no heartlessness: our friendship was healthy and rational; our regard mutual and honest, and I was forced to confess at last that there were, indeed (after all my sad experience to the contrary), true-hearted women in the world. I had no other alternative,

however, but to follow out my original plan of
travel, and hope for better things. So I and my
companion went to Vevay and Lauterbrunnen :
thence walking over the Bernese Alps we reached
at last the pretty city of Lucerne. From this
point we spent a night on the 'Righi : ' and in the
evening, at the miniature inn on the summit, I
spied, among the group of guides who were talking
together, the very courier who had been with my
dear English friends through Switzerland, and
whom I remembered was conversing with Miss
Grey on the occasion of my first visit to her hotel.
It was the work of but a moment for mutual recognition, and from him I heard most grateful news
concerning the object of my solicitude. 'Frantz'
described to me her precipitate departure, and the
terrible state of sorrow into which the sad news
had plunged the whole party.

" He showed me a watch and several other trink-
ets which the young ladies had given him when he
left their service, and told me, what I prized the
most to hear, that ' mad'moiselle, the one with the
large mild eyes, monsieur, had told him that, if he
ever saw monsieur, to explain to him the dreadful
circumstances of their sudden departure, and also
to bid him good-by for her and *au revoir.*'

" And this was all the comfort I got, and this is
all the comfort I 've had these many weary months
which have passed away since the precious idyl at
Martigny was so rudely broken up ; yet in my

dreams and waking moments, I am comforted by
that little word 'Toujours.' 'Toujours,' which ever
sounds in my memory.

"One night, in Paris, as I reached my apart-
ments, I found, lying on my table, this telegram:

"'TAMWORTH, ENGLAND, *November* 19, 187—

"'We all start for America by the Cunarder of
the 21st.   TOUJOURS.'

"'They have already gone,' said I, 'for to-night
is the 22d of November.' I could bear the suspense
no longer, and as soon as I could arrange my affairs
I felt impelled, as if by some hidden influence, to
follow them. And I *have* followed them, sought
them in all the principal cities of this great Union,
out to Colorado and down to Florida; and now
here I am in this checker-board city, so friendless,
so forlorn, so very, very ill.

"Heaven be praised for one crumb of comfort
which has just this moment arrived to illumine my
otherwise sunless lot. This little letter has followed me from place to place, and, by the same
relentless fate which has pursued me so long, has
never quite reached me, until it finds me ill and
despairing. Will it prove mere irony, a mockery of
words, and, like Moses of old, shall I only behold
the land of promise, and be deprived the happiness
of crossing a Jordan to possess it?

" ' NEW YORK, *July* 17, ——.

" ' We have just heard you are in this country, as we are about to reëmbark for England. Do come back to Tamworth, and hear the little adventure I promised to tell you in confidence, in the vale of Martigny.   TOUJOURS.'

" If there is strength enough remaining I start to-night, but " —

When Mr. Douce had finished reading, the effect produced upon his listeners was evidently not altogether favorable.

" I was hoping," said Hildegarde, " that that poor fellow was at last to be happy."

" Remember," said Mr. Douce, " that this is a true story, not a romance."

" I know it," replied Hildegarde ; " but is there

nobody happy, then? Good gracious! I was flattering myself that *I* was the only wretched creature in this world. Grief is getting to be altogether too common nowadays."

"Happy," answered Mr. Douce, "of course there *are* creatures who are happy: there are the May-bugs, for instance."

Mr. Worthington remarked "that this poor gentleman did have one crumb of comfort at last."

"A pretty dry crumb, though, and one which never sustained him sufficiently to get over to England to his girl," said Lawrence.

"There is always something which steps in just as one is about to grasp what one has been aiming at all of one's life, and dashes it away," sighed Miss Lucy.

"Just hear that youngster! One would think she had met with some great disappointment."

"Well, I don't believe," continued Miss Lucy, "there is anybody living who hasn't suffered in this way, young or old."

"That's what makes some of our characters so lovely, my dear," replied Lady Angela.

"It's inscrutable to me," said Mr. Douce, "how disappointments can possibly improve a body's character. I hate them now as heartily as ever I did when I was in petticoats, and I believe if I had never had any, my temper would have remained as angelic as it is."

"Yes, just about," said Angela, laughing.

" I'm sorry for the poor fellow, too ;" said Miss Brown, "for somehow I can't get him out of my mind. I don't see why Edith Grey didn't find him, and he her, and they both become happy 'like sensible people.'"

"And get married," said Hildegarde.

"Yes, and get married," said Miss Brown.

"And live in England in fine style."

"Yes, and — but why *did n't* they, do you think ?"

"Because," said Mr. Donce, "this is a *true* story and not a romance, and that's why."

CHAPTER V.

THE little circle of friends in Paradise was interested in regard to the way in which Mr. Cynicus Douce proposed to treat the subject of his lecture. Opinion was about equally divided,—some holding that he would surely discover a humorous side to it : and the other, that he would not. As Mr. Douce possessed a mind in which the sublime and the ridiculous were in close juxtaposition, the chances for either view were about equal.

A pleasant feature of life in the country is, that the miniature community becomes excited over every subject, large or small, which for the moment happens to occupy its attention. Whatever the ripple may be, temporary enthusiasm prevails until something fresher takes its place. So it was in this instance.

"Our Dual Individualities," said little Paradise ; " what on earth is the meaning of that ? "

The news had even reached the country store : and one old farmer remarked that he heard "Squire Douce was going to speak ' to the Hall' and show

how he and the rest of the boarders had another
body inside of 'em," and " for his part he believed
they had, for the way they acted the fourth 'July,
looked a leetle as if they all saw double."

The young people perceived at once that the
topic was too dry for them, and determined to
keep away from the Hall on Wednesday night.

Mr. Douce himself was quite perplexed as to his
best method of procedure. He did not mean to
"back out," after promising to write his views on
the subject ; but the truth was, he had no views at
all upon it. Still, to carry out his purpose, it was
imperative to have some sort of theory on which
to start his lecture. He therefore went out into a
neighboring lot, several evenings before the one
appointed, in order to ruminate upon the matter
and endeavor, if possible, to lay out a train of
thought which he could carry to a logical conclusion.

He found this no easy task, and as the time approached he became more and more nervous in his
action and appearance. He was forced to absent
himself from the pleasant coterie assembled on the
piazza, in order to complete his herculean labor,
and he subjected himself to all manner of good-
natured jokes as he flew from his writing to his
meals, and from his meals to his writing again.

" Heavens ! " said his friends on the hill, " how
relieved we shall all be when Cynicus has delivered
himself of that horrid lecture."

"And delivered us of it as well," said his friend Lawrence, with a mischievous smile.

"I trust," remarked Lady Angela, good-naturedly, "that our friend will never attempt such a subject again. He will surely die in the effort, for *thinking* always tells upon him fearfully."

"We must applaud him to the echo, even if he fails," said the kind-hearted Amelia.

"And throw flowers at him, in any event — but there he is," said Miss Brown, as the gentleman in question passed over the lawn with a large roll of papers under his arm. "How far have you got, Mr. Philosopher?"

"You see just how far," replied Mr. Douce, laughing, as he came to a sudden stand-still, and wiped his brow. "If I told you any more, you would never come to hear me."

"Will your lecture be 'illustrated?'"

"I may put in several cuts for some of my friends?" replied Cynicus, as he went on his way rejoicing.

The evening came and Mr. Douce was at his post in white cravat. The heat was oppressive, but the friendly audience in front of him did not seem to mind it, for they fanned themselves into a lower temperature and greeted each other with catching good-humor. There is a peculiar sort of delight which steals over one as he seats himself in his allotted place in a public hall, and watches his friends as they trip past him, singly or in couples, to their respective places. The little nods and smiles and ecstatic recognitions going on all about produce a unique species of exaltation which no other joy quite resembles. And what is so delightful about it is, that "young men and maidens, old men and children," are equally affected by the same pleasing emotion.

Mr. Donce appeared well in evening dress, though pale, and somewhat ill at ease. After spreading out his MS. on the desk and sipping from a tumbler of water, he thus began : —

ADIES AND GENTLEMEN. — I trust you will bear with me this evening while I present a few remarks on the subject of 'Our Dual Individuality.'

"I claim to be neither philosopher nor metaphysician, and therefore I offer only practical observations, suggested from the stand-point of common, every-day thought.

"You will acquit me of a desire to usurp either the place or the principles of any school of ethics, because you are fully aware that I appear here simply in pursuance of a promise which I hastily made under the genial influence of friendly hospitality, and from no aspiring ambition of my own. (Here he sips the water again.)

"It is well, perhaps, that we should occasionally pause in our humdrum, every-day existence and ponder over subjects which, though actually beyond our reach, are constantly exerting a mysterious influence upon our lives. Such pauses, even if they settle nothing, have a tendency to divert the mind into more serious channels than it is wont to pursue, and, therefore, to strengthen its natural fibre.

"I will only add, that in consenting to be present this evening, you have the proud satisfaction of adding to the wasted exchequer of the 'Paradise Library Fund,' an object so dear to each one of our hearts. (Applause.) Ahem! Questions concerning the mysteries of mind and matter, and their subtle relations to each other, are unusually attractive to the human intellect. The laws of chance and causation have tried its mettle, while the 'Theistic Theory' and the doctrine of 'Immanent Finality' have stirred its deepest philosophical powers. I have wondered how it would affect the world if it could actually decide any one of these important questions. For instance, if it could both mathematically and scientifically demonstrate that there was either something or nothing left to us of our ancient creeds besides the ego-consciousness. Or if we had finally proved, either that molecules moved themselves, or that there was an active, intelligent force behind them, pushing them on, what effect would the settlement of these questions have upon the welfare of the world?

13

"The philosophic mind loves to burrow among
the roots of peradventure and the tangled fibres
of uncertainty. It revels in the clouds of dust
raised by its own digging; and it does not seem to
matter so much that anything is logically proved,
as it does that there is rich territory before it
into which it may continue to delve. But this is
only in conformity with a general law: for the
mind, like the body, is at its best when actively
employed.

"*Our Dual Individuality* is the subject of my
paper this evening. Although this theme has a
smack of the metaphysical and unintelligible about
it, it still will commend itself as a very common
and practical fact. And while I am free to confess that it deals with matters about which but little is known,—a feature, however, which must
inhere, of necessity, to all intellectual discussions,
—it still possesses the element of attractiveness,
for it pertains to our actual daily experience,—
which we talk about as if we knew whereof we
speak, which is pretty nearly as comforting as if
we did.

"Every one is aware that consciousness is that
attribute of our intellectual natures which allows
us to perceive what passes in our own minds. I
must not stop very long here for fear that somebody might ask, what right any one has to call that
a mind—as we understand the meaning of that
word—in which our *perception* tells us things are

passing : if the mind does not perceive this passage,
but leaves the perception to perform that office!
If this be true, I don't see the necessity of having
a mind at all, and I should rank consciousness, or
perception, far above it as the intellectual reser-
voir, and degrade the mind to a position even below
that of the liver or the spleen: for *they always*
know when anything is passing through *them*. But
I hurry on to say that, having shown the high position occupied by our consciousness, I would re-
spectfully make this inquiry : that if every healthy
individual has consciousness, what is there to prevent his having two, or even more, consciousnesses?
No argument can be advanced to prove that there
is anything to prevent it ; in fact he *has* two.
Proof of this is both self-evident and plentiful.
Before passing to this, however, I pause for an instant to indulge in a little hyperbole on these phe-
nomena within us.

"Two wonderful self-consciousnesses in the same
body! One perfect entity working, at one time in
accordance with another perfect entity : then again
at variance with it! One great soul-judge sum-
moning another great soul-judge before a court of
last appeal with no name! A man calling himself
before himself for judgment pronounced by himself
on himself! One good second thought condemning us for the commission of crime suggested by
one first bad thought! One bad first intention
withstanding to the death a single good intention,

interposed by one good second thought! This
entity in a bad man is a devil! In a good one, an
angel! But to resume: —

"And God said, in the book of Genesis, 'Come,
let *us* make man,' etc. 'Let *us*.' It seems by this
expression as though even Deity itself possessed a
dual consciousness; because I take it that the word
'God' means 'God, the Creator,' and has no reference to the Trinity.

"Shakespeare makes Laertes tell his sister
Ophelia, when speaking of Hamlet's love for her,
'If with too credent ear you list his songs' — 'Fear
it, Ophelia, fear it, my dear sister; and keep you
in the *rear of your affection*,' etc. So in the same
play, Old Polonius tells Laertes, 'To *thine own
self* be true,' etc.

"Again, St. Paul, in his Epistle to the Romans,
says in the well-known passage, 'For what I do I
allow not; for what I would, that do I not; but
what I hate, that do I.' 'For the good that I
would not, that I do.' 'For I delight in the law
of God, after the *inward man*; but I see another
law in my members warring against the law of my
mind,' etc.

"Thomas Carlyle, in his Reminiscences, somewhere in the remarks on Edward Irving, and while
speaking of his own indecision after one of his
returns to London, remarks, 'Another morning
what was wholesomer and better, happening to
notice, as I stood looking out on the bit of green

under my bedroom window, a trim and rather
pretty hen actively paddling about and picking up
what food might be discoverable. See! *I said to
myself.* Look, thou fool! Here is a two-legged
creature, with scarcely half a thimbleful of brains;
thou call'st thyself a man, with nobody knows how
much brain, and reason dwelling in it; and behold
how the one life is regulated, and how the other!
In God's name concentrate, collect whatever of
reason thou hast, and direct it on the one thing
needful.' Now if anything were needed to establish the truth of this proposition, such extracts from
the inspired writings and the utterances of wonderful men would be amply sufficient to prove the
existence of separate individualities residing in the
same person; two distinct egos, or else a double
automatic-acting one.

"These two personalities reason with each other,
wrestle with each other, and alternately gain the
mastery over each other, as occasion serves, or peculiar circumstances favor. Each ego may be said
to live in a state of independent dependence, and
inter-mutual antagonistic attraction upon and with
the other. It is a queer state to be in; but it is a
queer sort of possession to be possessed of any way.
It appears that nobody is without these two inner
governors. They complete one's moral identity in
this world, as much as one's aesophagus or liver do
his physical nature. Nor are these individualities
always antagonistic. They often appear to dwell

together in lamb-like alliance. Happy is the man
between whom and his 'own self' there is no variance, for the skies are bright and the grass is
green. His heart throbs on with a cheery pulse,
and the whole hue of life is the color of the rose.
Trouble begins only when the paths of these two
individualities diverge; when one insists on 'boss-
ing' the other, or of donning a mask and false
presentment, which the other just as stoutly per-
sists in pulling off. This *alter ego*, whether good
or bad, keeps itself well out of sight, and yet is
lodged somewhere within very easy call. We all
know just where its hiding-place is, although we
never disclose it,—no, not even to *ourselves*,—whatever that may mean. 'Says I to myself,' is what
we are all constantly saying; and often 'myself'
retorts upon us in a most unpleasant manner, telling us that we are liars, and Pharisees, and wretched
hypocrites, when, by the dumb show of our outward mien, we appear to the world just the opposite.

"It would hardly be right to call this twin-
brother conscience, because it acts so often in a
manner different from a judge of the moral sense.
It is merely our *other* self; that individuality which
does not appear on the surface. It may be a bad
self as easily as a good self, as our *real* desires may
be horrid and devilish. This hidden soul-machinery
is so complicated and kaleidoscopic in its action,
that we hate and loathe what we at the same mo-

ment endure and embrace. And such is the subtle
character of these two natures, that they make us
love to hate that which we hate to love, and yet do
love. And we find ourselves deliberately reveling
in scenes, and becoming prominent in actions, which
we are simultaneously condemning with the bit-
terest invective.

" It is almost laughable to hear philosophy claim-
ing to determine what the human mind can or
cannot conceive : when such harlequin performances and moral pancraticals as these are turning
and tumbling us about in the manner above suggested.

" It would be extremely amusing, if it were not
so mighty serious, to watch the tussles which these
two egos are continually having with each other.
The devils — if there are any — must be most interested spectators of these little skirmishes which
are ever going on within us. How excited they
must be to watch an individual get into heated argument, for instance, and in his warmth say exactly what he neither means nor believes : and how,
little by little, he finds himself in a false position :
then how pride and obstinacy rush out to bolster
him up, until he becomes absolutely ridiculous.
And then they see a little door open, and the man's
other self steals out and walks tiptoe up to him,
and whispers in his ear that he is a fool : that
everything he said was a lie, and he knew it was
when he said it. And then the man seizes himself

by his own mental coat-collar, and by the little short hair in his mental neck, which hurts so, and twitches himself off his feet, and hauls himself away into a corner, where he jounces himself down with considerable roughness, and leaves himself there — poor, degraded creature in his own eyes — to chew out the 'end of sweet and bitter fancy,' until his punishment is over.

"I would like to inquire how the doctrine of either molecular force or will-power can be applied to such case as this? Again, when any individual puts on a sanctimonious outward guise of innocence, having a deep, conscious, and inner intent of committing wrong, the working of this dual consciousness is well exhibited. Here the *alter ego*, the other self, is a bad self, and anything but the man's real moral sense. It isn't his conscience, for it doesn't condemn him; on the contrary, it spurs him on to exhibit this heavenly expression, this lamb-like air, for the *express purpose* of committing the crime. That is not conscience. Indeed, in such instances, we might almost say there were three consciousnesses at work. One, the conscious being who goes about with the sanctimonious expression. Second, the spirit within him prompting him to deceit, for an ultimate bad end in view; and the third, the little dried-up party in the rear — conscience, if you please — which is doubling its fist in his face, and is hurrying him onward toward a gibbet of his own making, and, upon which he voluntarily mounts, and insists upon hanging and choking to death.

"When I commenced these remarks I was greatly impressed with the probable fact that we had two distinct consciousnesses within us; but after writing all the above, the fearful thought arises whether, besides the consciousness that there are two distinct consciousnesses within us — making three, — the consciousness that we *have* the consciousness of two consciousnesses may not prove that we have four. This suggestion is so frightful, however, that I instinctively fly from its discussion." (Applause.)

(Mr. Douce takes a sip from his tumbler, wipes the perspiration from his brow, and starts on again.)

"As at first sight the whole question of consciousness or no consciousness, or of two consciousnesses, or of any number of consciousnesses, might easily be confounded with that cognate subject, entitled, 'Second Sight and Visions.' I shall avoid all such complications by quoting the language of another, who says: 'In the subjective reality of objective falsity lies the reasonable explanation of many of

the delusions that affect mankind;' which settles the question, as the duality of individuality is no delusion, and therefore does not come within the above category. I wish now most reverently to draw an illustration of Dual Individuality from the New Testament, and I desire to descant upon it with becoming decorum and propriety. The illustration which I adduce is the 'Temptation,' as contained in the Gospel narration.

"There is at the outset a great difficulty in determining whether, in the first place, the temptation was a contest going on between the man Christ, that is, between his earthly passions and human desires, and his other self, just as it might go on within the bosom of any other human being in like position; or whether this contest went on within the divine being—in his mixed character, that is, between the humanity and his divinity; or, again, whether either of these individualities, that is, the man or the God, had this struggle with the genius of Evil — with Satan himself in his bodily shape? As nobody can positively settle either of these propositions, it is perfectly allowable for me, and for the purpose I have in view, to choose one of them. I certainly shall assume, then, that the struggle was between the *humanity* of the prophet of Galilee and somebody, or some other force. I don't hesitate to do this, because I conceive that there would be no struggle at all, no sort of temptation, as we understand that word to mean, if the

Great Master was there in his divine character, for it would be an impossible thing to tempt Deity. It is inconceivable, therefore, to say that Deity was taken up into a high mountain by Satan and tempted, and is degrading to all divine attributes. There is one little difficulty however, just here, which arises from the fact that the Master expressly says, after each attempt of Satan, 'Thou shalt not tempt the Lord thy God.' The only way I can see out of this dilemma is that Deity was there as the *Man* — 'with like passions to ourselves,' and that this struggle went on within himself, just as it would go on within the breast of any other man; but he also *knew* and *felt* that there was *divinity* in him, which he never, however, brought to his assistance, in order to get rid of the tempter, but contented himself by simply notifying Satan of the great fact. Just here I would mention an objection which is sometimes made on this passage, that it is 'used by the Saviour as forbidding himself to tempt God, not as a reproof to Satan.' In reply, I would ask what ground has the objector to make such an assertion? The context certainly says in so many words, that the Saviour, in one of his replies to Satan, says, 'Thou shalt not tempt the Lord thy God.' Surely if he did not say this to Satan, no more did he address him when he said, 'Get thee behind me.' It is strained and far-fetched to make this passage represent Our Lord as talking to himself.

"From this stand-point, then, we have a beautiful illustration of dual individuality. For whether the struggle transpired wholly within his own breast or not, it was still a struggle between his *two* individualities: one telling him how magnificent it would be to rule — as a man — all the kingdoms of the earth. How flattering it would be to self-love and vanity to receive worldly applause and popular adulation; and that he had only to accept the tempting offer, in order to establish an earthly and princely kingdom, — and this was a sore temptation to a poor carpenter's son. The other self was, we may imagine, at the same time whispering to him the words of the prophet: 'Vanity of vanities — all is vanity.' To yield now would be an ignominious finish to the glorious doctrine but yesterday promulgated in the streets and by-ways of Judea, a pitiable answer to the startling words of John the Baptist, 'Behold the Lamb of God!'

"The man battled with himself, weighing and balancing the arguments for and against, as they were brought up before him, and thanks be to an Almighty power, his better consciousness prevailed, and saved a world.

"Now, for a moment, let us take the other case, — that of Satan himself. Let us conceive for the nonce, that the Genius of Evil — if there be any such individual — appeared to the author of Christianity and presented to him his side of the question in the most attractive and dazzling manner.

We may imagine that he came with seductive mien — 'as an angel of light.' This outward appearance of innocence, and this persuasive language would naturally give the impression of a creature of honest purpose, possessing at the same time the charms of a commanding intelligence; while behind this fascinating exterior was lurking that other self, that earthly, sensual, and devilish individuality, reeking with direful and deadly purpose. Here the two egos are again displayed in sharp relief, one against the other,— that which first appeared, all smiles, blandishments, and seduction, and that other malignant principle, that quintessence of hell, which, had it won the victory, would have entailed upon the world inconceivable woe.

"I now pass to some animadversions of my subject, and will enumerate certain thoughts suggested by my theme, as they present themselves before me. It is a rare privilege, that of expressing one's self before a lenient audience without incurring responsibility; and I take advantage of this immunity to say that dual individuality is sufficiently a fact not to be seriously controverted, which leaves me at liberty to consume the remainder of my time in making general remarks upon my subject.

"The evolution of thought is never a contemptible process. On the contrary, it is a noble mental operation. The value of these mental products, however, is another question. This factor is determined by the fibre of the mind, whatever that vague expression may mean. Some thoughts, like some milk, are thin and watery; others are loaded down with the heavy cream of cogitation; so that it is not every thoughtful person who evolves the deepest and most valuable results by any means.

" The first thought on the subject of dual consciousness which I desire to express is rather a meagre one, but I note it down as a physician does a symptom.

" A good deal is told us by the superstitions, about the mystic significance of the odd number Three; but it occurs to me how much more might be said of the even number Two. Throughout the animal world duality in some of its forms seems to reside. Hearing, seeing, smelling, walking, talking, and feeling, — all require a duality of action of some sort in order to their exact performance. Even in thinking, or in living, or departing from this world, the soul and the body are necessary to its perfect execution. Besides the double ear, eye, nostril, tonsils, we have the leg, the vocal chords, with the dual action of the tongue with the roof of the mouth in order to taste. We have also the double lung, the two ventricles of the heart, the stomach and viscera for perfect digestion; the subtle conjunction of nerves and brain, the cerebrum and the cerebellum, the mystic tie between soul and body, the equally mystic loosing of soul from body, the male and female, the marriage tie; besides the marked antithesis throughout all nature between one thing and some other directly opposite, as light and darkness, good and evil, loss and gain, etc. Then ascending higher in the scale, the connection between the finite and the infinite, God and man, the highest ideal man a purified soul in a purified body, the perfection of heaven, Christ and his Church, and the perfect reconciliation, God and mankind, etc., etc.

"The next thought I wish to express is, that the very presence within us of this wonderful consciousness, whether it be single or double, or even triple; or whether it be only the varying shades of one and the same conscience; this fact, that there is inside every man, lodged in his brain, or outside of him, or wherever it may be, a subtle power — not subject to the same law of government as his vitals are, and not amenable to the same rule as his life, but which talks with him, argues with him, flatters him, makes him sin, causes him to repent, blanches his cheek with fear, accuses him of crime and drags him to a mental prison, — is a convincing proof of his immortality.

"It matters little whether molecules move themselves or not; it is certain that thought and passion move about at the bidding of some higher potentate, some invisible king. So intangible, so imponderable, and so invisible are they, as to pass beyond and reach into another sphere, differing from that which feeds man's body, and is compelled to witness man's ignoble actions. God — or whatever we may call the intelligent omnipotent First Cause — linked himself or itself to humanity, and made a domicile therein in this mysterious manner.

"These individualities are the God-principles, the seals of divinity, the heavenly brands of ownership set upon humanity, and I verily believe on some species of animals, and labeled them for heaven. They are seeds from a celestial country, planted in man to aid him to grow up from out of earthly degradation into an eternal existence.

"The next thought which I suggest is, that if it is true that this dual individuality in man, this *alter ego*, is sometimes good and sometimes evil, how is it possible that it can subserve the high aim of working out man's ultimate salvation?

"Vital principles, whose end is immortality, must of necessity be immortal themselves. It is rather contrary to modern thought to hold that the principle of evil is eternal, so, if these two principles within us, which are to accomplish such results, are immortal, — and they must be immortal to effect this, — then it follows that the bad principle must always be bad, eternally bad.

"The way I solve this rather difficult question in my own mind is this: That although it may be true that these individualities are immortal, it does not follow that the good individuality may not be a *stronger* principle than the *bad* one; and that, in the countless ages the great warfare might not end in the triumph of right.

"The next thought is: If the *bad ego* is immortal, how is it possible to overcome him? In two ways. One is: The badness of the one may not have been inherent, and, therefore, might in the end be overcome: leaving him, to be sure, without occupation, a rather discouraged sort of an individuality: a kind of an immortal drone, in the heavenly kingdom, minus his power to accomplish an evil. The second way is: That the doctrine and spirit of Christianity, acting in conjunction with the natural love of right implanted in every creature, might convert the other individuality at last, and so enable the man to attain eternal happiness: his very bad individuality becoming at last a very good one, and merging into the other, thus making him twice as good."

The audience here commence to grow weary and twist about in their seats, which causes Mr. Douce to say, quickly:—

"In conclusion, and before leaving the subject in your hands for discussion and decision, I wish to express my own thorough belief in the truth of my proposition: but also to add, that man's intellect is at best but feeble, and therefore, possibly I may have been, after all, greatly mistaken about this subject, and what I have been calling the duality of individuality is nothing more than our old friend conscience acting the part of Harlequin and assuming all sorts of quaint and disturbed forms in order to deceive us.

14

"Whatever may be the truth, there is undeniably something very mysterious and wonderful about this double mental machinery, which defies our comprehension."

(Mr. Douce bows his head low to signify that his lecture was concluded. Prolonged applause.)

When the audience separated they seemed to be considerably mixed up and confused in their notions of dual individualities. Some thought they had two, while others believed the whole idea was "moonshine." The lecture had one good effect, however, for it set Paradise thinking, and that is what Paradise needed.

The night was quite dark, and Cupid and Psyche (two lovers from the "Hill-top") decided to walk home together under cover of the deep shadows; so as they trudged along down the south road, hand in hand, Psyche remarked to Cupid, somewhat alarmed: "My dear, do you believe that you and I have dual individualities?"

"We may have *two* of them *now*, my darling," answered Cupid as he stole his arm about his inamorata's waist, "but next fall, after Bishop Good pronounces the benediction, we shall only have one."

"How queer it will all seem!"

"Yes — queer — but so comforting!"

"Still, I don't quite understand yet," said Psyche.

"Let me explain then, dearest," replied Cupid.

.   .   .   .

"It is perfectly clear to me now," whispered Psyche, as she tore herself from her lover's embrace and rushed up-stairs to her room in the new cottage.

CHAPTER VI.

MR. CYNICUS DOUCE SURRENDERS.

A LARGE room on ground floor in "Benjamin's" house; neat cottage furniture; elegant portière, and lace curtains gracefully concealing, within a deep recess, what might contain wash-stand and toilet apparatus; a gay-colored cretonne lounge; a centre-table, covered with latest periodicals, pocket editions of "Lucile" and Mrs. Browning's "Aurora Leigh;" lady's writing-desk with dainty scented paper, etc.; unanswered letters lying about; a bunch of roses on table; large traveling trunk at side of room; pair of pale blue silk slippers at foot of lounge; a small draped mirror, with lady's toilet extravagances, manicure box, etc.; on a bracket in corner, several phials of medicine in disuse; heavy lace curtains to all the windows; the Beautiful N. E. discovered at full length on the lounge, with paper-cutter in hand reading; as she reads, she seems to meditate, stops, commences again; she is very prettily dressed, and has a wee bit of a mole under her right ear; time, four o'clock in afternoon; all the guests either asleep or driving.

There is a saying that all roads lead to Rome; so in human society all things point to matrimony. I mean by matrimony a natural affinity of the sexes, which inevitably draws them together. Not that everything ends in marriage by a "long shot;" but, if matrimony were a big show, the tide of society would be seen setting in towards it from all quarters.

We do not all get into this matrimonial ring, and many who do want to get out again; but for all that, the fact remains, of this steady current flowing in the direction of the phantom tents of "union;" in spite of man's declaration to the contrary, and woman's pretensions to be above its influence. There are a few specimens from both the sexes who seem to be beyond the pale of this influence. For instance, there is the man-woman, that is, a female who has mixed up in her composition a sufficient number of manly attributes to supply the natural desire which each sex has for that which the opposite one possesses. Then, there are a few persons whose intellectual nature is far in excess of the affections, and which has squelched, so to speak, those inherent qualities of dependence, gregariousness, and love which are common to both sexes, and which constitute the charm of human society.

And lastly, there are those people who have once
been married, and whose self-will is so strong, and
the enjoyment of that sweet-boon "liberty" is so
delectable, that they cannot brook the mutual self-
sacrifice which such an alliance necessitates. But
even these poor seeming exceptions to the rule are
continually getting into trouble caused by this
same tendency of the sexes to affiliate.

Although Mr. Cynicus Donce did not exactly
come within the category of either of these classes,
he still professed to be beyond and above the common rules which regulate men. He had a kind
heart and a level head, and he saw, or thought he
saw, that all men were,—if not "liars," as the
sacred writer has it,—at least, dissemblers, back-
biters, unjust, slanderers, damners with faint praise,
self-lovers, shams, and Pharisees. And he came
to the conclusion that he had no use for this sort of
society. His creed was simple, and so he felt no
sympathy with what seemed to him the mere tin-
sel of piety minus its substance. He used society
for the amusement it afforded him, and was content. Of course he believed that there was some
virtue and affection and true worth in everybody,
but he saw so much of the other animus in the
world that he became sick of it.

Much to his chagrin, he discovered that these
views were gradually begetting in him what might
be termed a cynical diathesis. He was puzzled
what to do about it. Naturally of a warm and

ardent disposition, he started on life's journey,
loving and asking for love in return. He soon
found, however, that men and women want to be
loved well enough, and will accept all of it you
care to give them; will seize with avidity all your
kind offices, and all your self-sacrifices for their
joy; and all your untiring efforts to procure for
them the "front seats" in this world, and to feed
them with the cream of its pleasures; but if you
happen to suggest that perhaps there is something,
some little thing, due to *you* for all this devotion,
this self-abnegation, this wear and tear in their
service, they will look in your face with blank astonishment. The idea of making any such return
never entered their minds. Their philosophy is
after this sort: say they, "If you love me truly,
you will give to me all these things; and make all
these sacrifices freely, not expecting any return.
True love is unselfish. True love asks but to die in
the service of its idol. As it is more blessed to give
than to receive, so we are allowing you to enjoy
that supremest of pleasures." In reply to this you
ask: "Don't you *ever* make any return for benefits
received?" If they answered truly, they would
say: "Never, if we can help it. We merely receive. We are the kings and the queens of society;
born to *receive* homage, not to *give* it. You are
our vassals, and you should be happy in serving us."

This kind of philosophy is sound enough, Mr.
Douce thought, if practiced among a nation of

slaves; but he argued, that in society as at present
constituted these monarchs should be pretty sure
of their thrones before they attempted any such
tyranny. So Mr. Douce found by experience that
he loved, and loved, and loved, hoping for a return
in kind, but found that his love fell on a dry and
parched ground, "where no water is;" so this dis-
covery taught him a lesson which he acted upon
intelligently. He laughed and joked in society.
He sipped its honey, and smelled its flowers. He
ate its fruit, and spat out its pits; and so gave up
all idea of ever granting his warm heart a holiday
again. He considered that organ beyond the reach
of profane hands. It was in this way that he
flitted in and out among his fellows. He still had
his friendships, as he used to have his loves. He
seated himself just within the glare of society, and
was delighted to behold its full coruscations af-
fecting the destinies of others, while he sat snugly
ensconced in a corner watching the result. Now,
albeit his fine experience had brought him to a
logical conclusion, it did not at all destroy the truth
of accomplished facts. A fact is a fact, whatever
else is false. For instance, that beauty will attract, is a fact perfectly incontrovertible. Fascination and natural affinity between two people,
will, under certain conditions, inevitably produce
certain results. A woman's smile and a woman's
word of promise will certainly produce a known
and acknowledged effect on man. Even supposing

the one and the other to be as false as Hades itself. Such is the certainty of accomplished facts.

Like the rest of mankind, Mr. Douce was fallible. And though he was cynical, he was nevertheless mortal, and therefore susceptible to the great facts of fascination and beauty. So one day, one salubrious afternoon, he walked into the presence of his dear friend, the Beautiful N. E., as a man of recognized and distinct convictions, and he walked out of it again soon afterwards, shattered in his convictions and riddled in his principles; and this is the way it happened: —

Time, that wonderful medicine, effects most astonishing cures. It eats up animosities; seals and shatters friendships; destroys youth; throws a film of uncertainty over its follies, and a glamour over its crimes. But among its beneficent and charming effects, none was more marked than that produced upon our beautiful friend, the "Nervous Exhaustionist."

Either the tonic air of Paradise, the gradual influence of her summer experience among normal people, or her own returning health, caused her to view life from a different stand-point — or rather reclining point of view — for she appeared one morning, to the astonishment of all her friends, mounted on a slashing bay mare with a banged tail, and commenced galloping over the Paradise hills in such a manner as to completely knock up her faithful man Thomas, and delight her loving family. This was no spurt or vagary, but she kept on in her change of purpose until all that was beautiful and glorious in her had been fully aroused from that long lethargy in which it lay buried, and she became at once the comfort and the pride of an admiring crowd of friends. The fact that his beautiful friend had taken her place again among what he termed "the powers of the earth," was

a source of intense satisfaction to Mr. Cynicus Douce. Knowing her from childhood, he felt there had been lost to the world a noble woman, who had gradually succumbed to the seductive allurements of a luxurious invalidism. His heart kindled with kindly emotion when he beheld what he was pleased to call her "resurrection," and he experienced a pardonable sort of self-gratification as he beheld this great change, which, he flattered him-

self, was the fruit of his own precious example and teachings.

Although Mr. Douce was unalterably fixed in his favorite creed concerning society, he became gradually convinced that two opposing facts could also exist, side by side, without detriment to either. For instance, although he firmly believed that the world was teeming with hypocrisy and selfishness, he was also beginning to allow that there was also such a thing in society as true love and disinterestedness. In this dubious frame of mind he left his room in the new cottage, and trudging over the green grass, knocked gently at the door of his fair friend, the Beautiful N. E.

(Knock heard at door.) N. E. hastily looks in mirror, adjusts her bangs, and pretty costume of lace and ribbons. Gets up and sits down again with left foot under her, and answers in a quiet, mellifluous voice, "Come in!"

(Enter Mr. Douce, a trifle excited.)

N. E. "How do you do, my friend?"

Cyn. "All the better for seeing you, — for I am miserable to-day."

N. E. "Why?"

Cyn. "The fact is, I have lately given myself up to pet theories and views on subjects which never seem to come out as I want them to."

N. E. "The best way, then, is to let them 'gang their own gait,' and not try to alter them. People *will* do as they please, in spite of you."

Cyn. "You're right. (Sits.) I never mean to raise a hand again to alter that which I see plainly is destroying society. The whole social body is rotten with selfishness. Let it go to Guinea for all me." (Here Mr. Donce puts both hands in both pockets and stretches both his feet out to their fullest extent.)

N. E. "The whole?"

Cyn. "Yes, man, woman, child, and dog. No! the dogs are *un*-selfish. I'll except the dogs!"

N. E. "Why, my friend, you are in an awful state to-day. Do try and look at things through a different colored glass. Don't forever pick out of your paint-box the indigo, and the bistre. Let's have a little light blue and *couleur-de-rose* once in a while, to give the picture a livelier tone. Just look at that water-color of mine! How do you like it?"

Cyn. "It's clever — very clever. Everything you do is clever. (Cynicus looks at the sketch through both his hands.) But I want you to accomplish something better than a faded, neutral-tinted, wishy-washy water-color. You have the capacity to 'set the world a-fire.'"

N. E. "But I can't do it, my friend!"

Cyn. "I say you *can*; but the trouble is, you are too rich, and too pretty, and too much busied about the shape of your nails, to have any time to save your fellow-men from going to the devil."

N. E. "Why, Cynicus Douce, you are crazy. You know very well that I am powerless to do what *you* want me to do."

Cyn. "No: you're not. You've got character enough in you to command the world's attention, and compel them to listen: but the modus is the trouble." (Here Mr. Douce shoves his hand through his short hair, and pulls out his collar from his throat, as if it were too tight for him.)

N. E. "The modus. What *do* you mean?"

Cyn. "I mean, as things are managed nowadays, the rich act as drags and hindrances rather than as pioneers of human progress."

N. E. (Carefully unstopping the Preston-salts bottle, and taking a whiff.) "It won't do to pooh-pooh the rich, especially rich women, for without *them* the rich *men* would never act at all."

Cyn. "Exactly! And the fault I find with rich

women is this: that while they recognize the need of reorganizing society by an example of thrift and self-denial, they are so often content to let this remain a mere sentiment, never acted upon."

N. E. " Perhaps you are right. Although I recognize the need of philanthropy, it is hardly natural for those who are mercifully removed from want and poverty to deny themselves the good things of this life." (Here she pulls a bursting rosebud to pieces, and eats the leaves.)

Cyn. " Excuse me!" (shoving his hand through his short hair again.) " It is incumbent on the influential members of society — those that are fully able to indulge themselves to the utmost — to set a noble example to the rest of the world. I have given up, however, all hope of reaching that coveted goal, for our richest women, those who ought to set this example, are the very ones who are sunk deepest in the slough of self-indulgence." (Looks at the Beautiful N. E. with sadness.)

N. E. " You mistake me, then, if you think that I am, for I have long felt convinced that there is something nobler in this world than the selfish study of one's own comfort. I seem to realize, for the first time, that I am only one out of three hundred millions of other mortals, who never heard of my existence." (The gray eyes of the N. E. glisten with emotion, and a rosy flush appears in her cheeks.)

Cyn. " Glorious! Superb! Now you make me believe that a woman is something more than an illogical quibble!"

N. E. "My dear Cynicus (with a comical smile), I hardly know what to make of this unusual compliment. It quite overwhelms me. Pray let me get used to it before you go on."

Cyn. "It's drawn out of me, in spite of myself; for it is the symptoms of your signal victory over the subtle weaknesses engendered by wealth and luxury, which you have shown of late, as well as for the noble sentiment you have just uttered, which fills me with admiration." (A pause.) "And, Madeleine, if you have overset all my preconceived notions of woman's frailties, you have also, suddenly, made me the happiest of men." (Madeleine blushes and bites end of fan.)

Mad. "Why, dear friend?"

Cyn. "I cannot tell why I am happy; but all I know is, that what you have just said has suddenly made me so. With these blemishes removed you become, in my eyes, the most noble of women. Now, can you — will you — I don't know what I am doing — but you *must know*, Madeleine, what I *mean*." (Visible emotion in both parties, with perceptible signs of a denouement. Silence for a few seconds, during which both principals insensibly approach each other.)

Cyn. "I am perfectly boyish about all this; but I can't help it, Madeleine. I love you; yes, adore you; worship the very ground you stand on. Now, what can you say to me?"

(Madeleine looks askance; hesitates a moment

to toy with her fan before she replies, with a roguish smile on her lips.)

Mad. "You may well ask me. What can *I* say? for I am truly astonished at what *you* say. You surely cannot be the same gentleman whose motto a moment since was, 'Vanity of vanities, all is vanity.' You cannot be that happy soul who denied the necessity of woman's society to man, and proclaimed his perfect freedom from all uxorial aspirations!"

Cyn. Ah, Madeleine! you have your revenge. I acknowledge that some of my conclusions have been erroneous."

Mad. "Yes: your philosophy has been of such a frightful sort that no sensible woman could ever think of — of — a man holding to such a creed in any other light than as a dangerous foe to her happiness: — that's my idea!"

Cyn. "You don't mean to say, then, you *hate* me?"

Mad. "I don't *hate* anybody. I only say that any mortal professing such a horrid creed would be a dangerous element to be admitted into a woman's life. *I* never could be happy with such a creature!"

Cyn. "Ah, Madeleine! you have known me from boyhood; and do you believe that I could ever hurt you?"

Mad. "You *have* hurt me often by what you've said, and by the way you've 'gone on.'"

Cyn. "And am I to understand that you never can love me? Great heavens! Are you going to break my heart?"

Mad. "My dear Cynicus, I'm no girl of sixteen; I have reached the sober years of discretion, and fully realize that no two people can ever be happy together who have not some identical interests, or who are not in a measure *en rapport*."

Cyn. "And don't you think that you and I are, in some 'measure,' *en rapport*? Have n't we been growing more so every day?"

Mad. "Have we?" (With a doubtful and dazed expression.)

Cyn. (Brushing a tear from his eye.) "Yes, we *have!* I know we have; I feel we have; and what are *opinions* after all, Madeleine? And what are conclusions, after all, in the face of an actual, unbiased, and true-hearted affection? Madeleine, I love you. Do you fully understand what that means? Not a make-believe, namby-pamby love; not a fanciful sort of partiality, but a gradual, mature, and healthy passion, resulting from life-long experience and the growth of years!"

Mad. (Sighs.) "I understand, my dear friend, or I think I understand your feelings. The *revelation* of them is what astonishes me so much. I cannot surely be blamed for this astonishment; nor can you wonder at my hesitation to believe you. You have taught me for so many years to think of you in any other light than the one in which you

now display yourself, that I have great difficulty in
realizing that what I hear is not a dream of fancy,
or one of those exhibitions of hollowness in which
you think the world indulges so much."

Cyn. "Oh, don't be cruel, friend of my youth.
You have heretofore seen me as a quasi philosopher;
but you now behold me robbed of it all — a mere
child again."

Mad. "Alas, my poor friend! Do I understand
that you now avow all this fine argument about the
'emptiness of life' to be only just so much nonsense, and not your real opinion after all?"

Cyn. "Oh, pity me! pity me, dearest love! for
I really do confess that there is such a thing as
true affection; I feel it too deeply not to believe
in its existence. My only mistake has been in
going too far with my philosophy."

Mad. "Do you then recant, my friend, and give
up all these fine-spun theories?"

Cyn. "No, dearest Madeleine, not all, not all;
spare me a few! For I cannot entirely disbelieve
a conclusion which many eventful years of experience and trial have brought me to. No, not all!
I do believe that this world, by itself, is well enough;
that honesty, truth, and virtue, unlet and unhin-
dered, would thrive and flourish here; but that the
degenerate results of our modern civilization have
plated, so to speak, everything and everybody with
a thin veneer of falseness and pretense. This con-
viction I can never surrender."

Mad. "How is it then possible for *this* to be true, and at the same time your love for me to be equally a truth?" (Madeleine looks serious, and straightens the feathers at the top of her fan with thumb and forefinger.)

Cyn. "I don't know *how* they can be true. I only know they *are* true, nevertheless. Isn't it possible, dearest child, that the world should be filled — no, not *entirely* filled, because I've given up that point — but a *good deal* filled up with hypocrisy and humbug: and also be true that I, the cynic and the dis-believer, should love and adore you? I should like to know why both of these truths can't exist at the same time on the earth? Why? Tell me why can't they?"

(Mr. Douce here furtively takes the left hand of the Beautiful N. E., who passively allows it to be held undisturbed.)

Mad. (With hesitation.) "I have sometimes thought, Cynicus, that — that perhaps — you were about half right in some *few* of your conclusions. But I never could *acknowledge* it, you know, never;

my womanly instincts would n't allow me to do *that.*"

Cyn. (With effusion.) " I don't ask you, dearest, to agree with my theories: I only pray that you acknowledge my *facts.* Do you, can you believe, that when I swear I love you, I say the solemn truth?"

Mad. (Looks a little more shaky than she did, slight twitchings descernible at the corners of her pretty mouth: she sighs.) " I believe you."

Cyn. " Can you then permit this fact, which you say you believe to be true — will you permit it to remain unaccepted?"

Mad. " It makes me both happy and frightened to acknowledge this avowal as a fact."

Cyn. " Then, dearest Madeleine, will you not give me the inexpressible delight of hearing from your own lips that that love finds an echo in your own dear heart?"

Mad. " I find it impossible to tell you *what* I feel."

Cyn. " I won't ask for words then, darling! Look it. Tell me with your dear eyes that you reciprocate my love!"

(The Beautiful N. E., after several vain attempts, at last looks the friend of her youth straight in the eyes, while two large tears roll down her pale cheeks.)

The pearly, waning sunlight was the only witness of this momentous contract, — shedding upon the two a loving, silent benison.

Tableau-Vivant.

So let all Nervous Exhaustionists and Pessimists perish!

WHAT THE WORLD SAID.

As may be supposed, when the engagement between the Beautiful N. E. and Mr. Douce was announced, all Paradise was agog with excitement. The very day and the very hour when the important event occurred was, by some wonderful means, known to the little community almost as soon as the event itself had become a certainty. Her intimate friends immediately resolved themselves into a committee of the whole " to discuss the subject." Some said, " I told you so. I knew that something

must come out of all that apparent disagreement
and yet constant intimacy." While others remarked. "They will be a dreadfully unhappy
couple; for when a spoiled child and an old bachelor come together, look out for breakers!" The
young ladies were very much interested in the daily
progress of the match. The children reported to
the grown people every time either of the engaged
parties moved a muscle which might be construed
into an amatory evidence, while the old heads wondered how it all came about.

The great question which agitated everybody
was, "Is this the result of persistence on Mr.
Douce's part; the end of a faint-heart-never-won-
fair-lady policy; or did it happen naturally, as
people take measles, or the mumps?" There was
one very wise person upon the Hill who delivered
quite an oration on the subject. He remarked, "I
believe that Cynicus Douce never would have asked
the Beautiful N. E. to marry him, had it not been
for just the peculiar state of circumstances which
happened to surround him on that particular morning, and at the very moment. I believe," said this
person, "that he had no more idea of being engaged to his life-long friend *then*, than at any other
time within the past ten or fifteen years; and it
only proves that all these things are ordered for us.
It shows that, work as we will in one direction or
another, 'there is a divinity which shapes our
ends.'"

" Some men think that by constantly belaboring
a woman, and sending flowers to her, and asking
her to marry them over and over again, that at
last she will succumb, and accept the persistent
adorer. This may, once in a while, be the case,
when the man is very, *very* rich, and all *her* family
are poor, or she herself is getting a little — a wee
bit *passée*. But nine times out of ten this is not
so. If a woman is inclined to dislike a man, why,
she dislikes him, that's all; and if she likes him,
she likes him, and also every foolish thing he says,
and every idiotic thing he does. Another man,
really twice as fascinating, and twice as wise, may
try to step in and 'cut him out;' but all the pos-
turing, all the flowers, and the Jacqueminot buds,
and all the 'taffy and the caramels' in the world,
are entirely thrown away upon her. They are not
worth, in the mind of this infatuated one, a scin-
tillation of the value which she attaches to one
miserable faded leaf which 'her Alphonse' may
have given her, or to an awkward expression of admiration which he may have awkwardly expressed.
Now Cynicus Douce did not think or know anything about his love for the Beautiful N. E. I
believe he supposed that she and he were to be
just as they had been to each other, — good friends,
you know, to their life's end; but feeling rather
blue that morning, and being so pleased with Madeleine for her 'perking up' and flying round on
horseback, and so delighted with what she had told

him about her new sort of feeling on subjects which had so interested him all his life,—that he suddenly felt a strange impulse to tell her that he loved her for it, and then the ball was opened, and there was nothing to be done but go right ahead, and that's the way, in my opinion, this affair came about."

Now this person was pretty nearly correct in his view of that important event. At any rate the thing was done, and the world was already getting used to the new arrangement.

Autumn had now commenced to admonish the fair sojourners that the big trunks must again be packed, and thoughts be turned once more towards the bustle and the stir of city life. Maids and mistresses were half buried in mountains of immaculate linen, which lay in heaps on the floor, while the great towering "three-deckers" stood gaping by, ready to swallow them up at the appointed moment.

It is a sort of melancholy occasion, this breaking up of a summer's campaign, this end of a *dolce far niente* life. Especially so if these necessary arrangements happen to come on a morning when there is an unwonted balminess in the air, and a peculiarly lazy haziness over the landscape; when the turning leaves are exquisite in color, and seem to be silently murmuring mournful farewells.

One stops his packing, and, looking out from the

open window over the quiet hills, is tempted to ex-
claim : " No ! It 's impossible to leave all this love-
liness ! I *must* take that long desired drive to-day,
which I have been so often about to take, but have
never quite accomplished." Time, however, waits
for no man. To-morrow becomes to-day, and to-
day yesterday, almost while we are looking from
the lattice over the glowing landscape. The big
wagon is already at the door, and they are calling
upon us to take our places. Before we quite know
we are off, the puff-puff of the great locomotive
carries us swiftly behind the hill, shutting out from
view the scene of so many delights.

Yes, the summer is past ! As we go clattering
and banging along the iron track, each moment is
separating us farther and farther from the almost
ideal existence in which we have been dreaming ;
and is hurrying us nearer to those tentacles of
worry and toil with which the great metropolis
in front stands ready to enwrap us.

One shrill whistle and two shorts " toots " are
sufficient to bring us again face to face with the
city and all its cantankerous cares. Friends are
everywhere on the streets nodding recognition and
welcoming our return. The furnace fires must
soon be lighted. Our ulsters and mufflers taken
from the camphor-trunk, and presto ! in a twink-
ling, the scene is so completely changed that the

summer which has but now departed may just as
well be the summer of ten years ago, as the one
whose influence is still showing itself on our brown
and ruddy cheeks, and in our vigorous gait.

THE glimpse of life's comedy which we have
taken in the foregoing chapters is but an incom-
plete and partial view of that daily drama which
goes cheerily on in the life of society.

The characters which have appeared are meant
to be merely types of real people; while what
they have said is a chance echo of opinion, enter-
tained by friends at our elbow. These people and
these opinions may not be exactly those to be found
everywhere, yet, we think, such can easily be discovered without the aid of a telescope. As the
world is both larger and smaller than we realize it
to be, so there are persons in it who take narrower
and broader views of the questions of the day than
we naturally expect they would. One charm of

life is disagreement. The curse of it is when this disagreement carries rancor and personality. Expurgated of these baleful elements, existence would resemble a bouquet of varied and exquisite flowers. The doleful and pessimistic opinions of Mr. Cynicus Donce may be pronounced both unnatural and strained, yet there are many good people of one's acquaintance who hold ideas akin to those expressed by him, and who can say just how far Mr. Donce was wrong. The peculiarly delicate case of the Beautiful N. E. may be dismissed as an exaggerated form of an unheard-of disease, if such a thing is possible, yet there are many individuals in real life who are afflicted with a complaint very similar to that which laid our fascinating friend on a couch of delicious pain.

The healthy tone of Lady Angela's mind may possibly be thought to be more in accordance with that of every-day people, and yet there are not a few, I trow, who, if they cared to think at all on the subject, would quarrel with just that frankness of expression which characterized this lady's speech.

In this world each one is apt to take *himself* for a standard of virtue and godliness, and think that this or that thing is neither natural nor right, simply because he or she would never think of doing thus and so. To prove this, propose any question of every-day experience to a company of men and women, and observe how naturally they decide it in accordance with a view favoring their own line of conduct under such circumstances, rather than what would be the actual truth of the matter. For instance, tell a lady that her sex have two objects in adorning themselves, — one, expensively, to please their own vanity; the other, becomingly, to fascinate the other portion of humanity, and she will reply that it can't be true, as *she* never does either the one or the other. Tell a man that the world is happy when some poor devil "comes to grief," and he will say that it can't be so, because *he* never felt so himself; forgetting entirely that a *soupçon* of that same emotion was present in his heart but yesterday.

It would be tedious to pursue this subject farther; for, however interesting the theme, man is so constituted as to be unable to bear but little of one thing at one time. Nothing but "Robinson Crusoe" and "Gulliver's Travels" can be read forever.

It remains for us to say a few words, by way of valedictory, concerning the fate of some of the friends who have occupied our attention throughout these pages.

The Beautiful N. E. is living as the radiant and contented wife of Mr. Cynicus Douce. Her wealth ministers to do good where good can best be done. Her aristocratic yet unpretentious home is the arena where wit, philosophy, and elegance vie with each other in friendly strife. Nothing mawkish or unreal thrives in her society; while everything lovely and lovable, generous and beautiful, finds a welcome there. She has shown to the world that "Beautiful N. E's," all over the country have only to shake off the luxurious lethargy which lugs at their life, in order to become endeared and honored members of a thankful society. Cynicus and she are a thoroughly charming couple. They live like sensible people, and so get on famously together.

In addition to all their other fine qualities, they possess that wonderful, ever-to-be-prized, matrimonial desideratum, called tact. If there could only be more tact and less money in the world, everybody would be happier. Tact is more valuable than solitaire ear-rings or ancestral coaches; and more to be prized in a family than dresses from Paris, or an eligible match. These two delightful friends have a "large assortment" of the above-mentioned article, hence the resultant happiness which fills to running over their cup of domestic joy.

Now a word concerning their intimate companion, the Lady Angela. She is so like everybody else, and yet so very unlike, that everybody loves her; selfishly imagining they see in her what they *think* they possess themselves. She is an admired object of the society in which she moves, because she is, not only on a level with every-

16

body else's good qualities, but also far above every-body else, in the same direction.

Natural and elegant, unsuspicious and clever, childlike, and even manlike, she can but challenge admiration, and inspire respect. It is a very elevating circumstance to be the friend of a healthy, clever, and thinking woman : one who can stand up in argument against a full-grown intellect, and do good battle with it. There is something very inspiring in this condition of things. The Lady Angela does all this effectually. What she knows she knows exactly. What she says, she means. What she proposes to do, she does. The Lady Angela does n't joke, though she is the opposite from solemn. She merely says "yes" when she means "yes," and "no" when she means what that mono-syllable implies. The idea of "badinage" is a stranger in her direct mind : she laughs and romps and "skylarks" to any extent, but if she makes an appointment she keeps it. If she says she is going anywhere, it is no "moonshine;" she goes somewhere. At school, there was always some unlucky scholar in love with her. She belongs to that class of her sex which have girl-lovers as well as man-lovers. But the Lady Angela, with all her infantile sprightliness, is in reality only a lovely tyrant. Her adorers, both male and female, are abject adorers : given over to her interest — body, soul, and opinion. She has a way of extract-ing from them their entire allegiance, without being

called upon to furnish any of her own in return;
accustomed thus to *receive*, all her life, she naturally forgets to give. If one is a receiver only, he
soon loses the impulse to give. So it is, in some
degree, with the Lady Angela. Her lovers insist
on loving her, and pouring into her lap all their devotion, and find it so very agreeable that they
forget, until it is too late, to obtain anything from
her in return. But it is a boon indeed when the
Lady Angela does actually " smile back," or give,
as she sometimes does give, "a *quid pro quo*." On
these happy occasions it is as if Juno had smiled
in the council of the gods.

It was pure good fortune that Mr. Douce and
his Beautiful N. E. lived so near, in the great city,
to their friend, the Lady Angela. Their dinner-
parties and other entertainments, at each other's
houses, were never complete unless all three were
together, so that the society of the metropolis was
pretty nearly "perfect" when this was the case.

It may be asked, "Was the Lady Angela married? And if not, why not?" History is a little
vague on this point. Some people thought she had
once lost her heart, and then got it back again;
another portion were not quite so sure. Certain it
was that she broke men's hearts from sheer ina-
bility to do otherwise; and if her own was not
shattered, it was because she never met the man
worthy of performing such a redoubtable feat of
arms.

Something should now be said concerning the little church in Paradise, and its new rector. The miniature excitement which raged in the parish during the summer, in its efforts to obtain what it desired, at last culminated in success. The Rev. George Faxon is a model priest, meeting every requirement which such a person is expected to possess. In the first place, he is an intelligent, level-headed gentleman ; next, he is a conscientious, honest Christian. Then again, he possesses tact, talent, and coolness. Besides all these fine qualities, he is benevolent, lenient, and trustworthy. Travel, and a good deal of knocking about, has given him liberality of view, and a lot of sturdy principle. His sermons are twenty-three minutes long. He preaches what St. Paul preached, and does not busy himself in trying to explain the unexplainable ; or talking about that which he knows nothing at all.

He is thirty years old, and charms every variety of Christian in his parish, from Mr. Cynicus Douce to Miss Eunice Smart. The weekly contributions have also steadily increased ; and from eight dollars and fifty cents, as of former years, they now amount to twenty-eight and twenty-nine every Sunday.

To cap the climax, Mr. Faxon is married. His wife neither talks too much nor tattles. She has " means " of her own, so her house is not wanting in those surroundings which make home so pleasant, and the parish feels more easy in regard to the salary question. Unlike most ministers, who usu-

ally fall in love with some damsel in the town
where the seminary is situated, before they are
raised to the priesthood. George Faxon waited
until he returned from Europe before he married.
His friends think he lost nothing by this delay.
In short, the minister and his wife are a couple,
such as any parish should be proud of. The sacred
profession is honored by a conscientious, honest,
and intelligent member, while the dear old church
has no worthier son to sustain her ancient prestige,
or bear aloft her sacred banner. George Faxon is
a handsome fellow, and his wife is not an invalid —
two weighty facts in a parish.

As to our other friends of whom we have spoken:
those who gathered together under "Benjamin's
pines" to listen to the "Diary of an Unfortunate
Gentleman;" who assembled in Paradise Hall
where Mr. Douce gave his lecture, and who passed
those happy hours on "Top-Knot" when the melons
were ripe, we are glad to say that "Paradise" still
claims them for her own. Indeed, "Paradise"
would hardly be "Paradise" at all, unless their
gladsome smiles and beaming countenances were
recognized amidst its emerald glades and undulating hills. What though they be but ideal companions in the realms of fancy, — still, to say farewell to even these, stirs within our heart a feeling
akin to that which is present when living friendships die. Let us hope that as the halcyon days
approach, and the robin and the bluebird fly back

from their southern homes, so these dear friends
may return each season in the puffing train which
stops at the little red-roofed station among the
green hills of "Tucit-Kennoc."

www.ingramcontent.com/pod-product-compliance
Lightning Source LLC
Chambersburg PA
CBHW030401270326
41926CB00009B/1216